Classes, Crises and Coups

Peter C. Lloyd

Classes, Crises and Coups

Themes in the Sociology of
Developing Countries

PRAEGER PUBLISHERS
New York · Washington

BOOKS THAT MATTER

Published in the United States of America in 1972
by Praeger Publishers, Inc., 111 Fourth Avenue,
New York, N.Y. 10003

Copyright © 1972 by Peter G. Lloyd

Library of Congress Catalog Card Number: 75–186467

Printed in Great Britain

Contents

197639

Preface

What is happening today *inside* the poorer nations of the world? We know of the continued poverty of their peoples and, as in the case of Vietnam and its neighbours, of the horrors of war. We ascribe these things in part, perhaps, to the political and economic relationships existing between these poor nations and those of the rich industrial West, and we experience feelings of guilt. But we know little of the social processes which are going on within the poor nations. In this book I shall try to describe some of them.

Our current ignorance is understandable if not necessarily excusable. The mass media provide us with little background material to the dramatic current events. A military coup may seem like a game of musical chairs played between power-hungry individuals; the underlying tensions in the society are understressed. Even when dramatic events are presented in an analytic framework, we are apt to endow the social categories used with the characteristics familiar to us in the West; for convenience we term the urban workers a proletariat and then expect a developed sense of class consciousness. In this way we are led more deeply into error.

We must look more closely at the types of society developing among the peoples of the poorer nations. In the following pages I have relied heavily both upon my own experience in West Africa and, for other areas, upon writers who have similarly spent considerable periods studying society as sociologists or social anthropologists. The resultant picture is one of kaleidoscopic variety; the conventional generalizations about modes and directions of modernization seem quite inadequate. But I offer no alternative generalizations. Our knowledge of the social processes involved is still too fallible for us to predict, for instance, that certain situations will give rise to tensions of such a degree as will lead to violence rather than conciliation. Again, the sociologist cannot rely solely on the theories emerging from his own discipline – he needs the assistance of the political scientist and the economist, and, perhaps the psychologist too, in order to evaluate those factors in which these scholars have greater expertise. My aim here is to illustrate, with examples drawn from Latin America, Africa and Asia, some of the themes which deserve greater attention.

My debts to mentors are so numerous that I cannot possibly list them with fairness. Those who have been kind enough to read the drafts of this book include John Rex, Adrian Peace, Riall Nolan and Henry Bernstein; I am grateful for their comments. To those who typed the book and edited it I owe a similar debt.

Brighton, Sussex   PETER C. LLOYD
February 1971

Moreover, we must recognize a new threat to the peace of the nations, indeed to the very fabric of society. We have seen in the last few years the growth of a cult of political violence, preached and practised not so much between states as within them. It is a sombre thought but it may be that in the 1970s civil war, not war between nations, will be the main danger we will face.

Edward Heath, British Prime Minister,
at the United Nations General Assembly,
23 September 1970

1 Introduction

September 1969. In a bloodless dawn coup in Bolivia the commander-in-chief of the army seized power while the president was touring in a distant part of the country. The president was given asylum in Chile. The general had been a leading figure in Bolivian politics in recent years and was seen as an aspirant to presidency in the coming elections. He seems to have feared the growing opposition to him of the Movimiento Nacionalista Revolucionario, the party founded by left-wing intellectuals which had governed the country from the revolution in 1952 until 1964. The general's popular support came from the Quechua Indians. On assuming power he described his new civilian and military government as left-of-centre. He immediately annulled the petroleum code, an act which was interpreted as a possible precursor to the nationalization of the American-owned oil industry; and he promised to consider the wage demands of the tin-miners. He had been active against the guerrilla bands of Che Guevara.

In India communal rioting broke out in the prosperous industrial city of Ahmedabad and over 400 people are believed to have lost their lives – a total which exceeded the total of such deaths in the previous three years. The trouble seems to have started with the desecration of a Hindu temple; but the Muslims, who form a quarter of the city's two million population, suffered most. Gandhi had lived in this city for almost twenty years and had set up his first community living centre here; but in recent years growing Hindu militancy and the organization of Muslims had heightened the tensions between the two groups.

In Nigeria the war between the Federal State and secessionist Biafra continued into its third year without any marked signs of an imminent conclusion. In the Western State over 400 farmers from villages around Ibadan had been jailed for failing to pay their taxes – an apparent protest against stagnant or declining living standards produced by the war economy and a poor cocoa harvest. A mob broke into their prison and released them. In the ensuing round up of the liberators and escapees by police and army fifty people were killed.

A few years ago we might have argued that events such as these were endemic to the poorer nations of the world and exemplified the backwardness of their populations. Today with battles between Catholics and Protestants in Northern Ireland, race riots in American cities and student rebellion in most of the industrial nations we are less certain of these differences between rich and poor nations. However, unlike the strikes of violence nearer home, the events in the poorer nations suddenly make the news headlines and then, as soon as calm returns, vanish again leaving us bewildered as to their antecedents and their consequences. But as each month brings new examples of coups and riots we do perhaps wonder whether violence is in fact on the increase or whether improved communications merely bring to our notice events which in earlier decades would have passed unreported. The prominence now given to them does however signify the concern felt by people in the industrial nations. Humanitarians deplore the heavy death tolls – though they less often question the costs in poverty and suffering of a stagnant society. Others fear that violence will impede rates of economic development by diverting resources to unproductive ends. As the Great Powers become involved through the supply of arms to the rival parties, as in Nigeria or Vietnam, global war seems to threaten.

The crises sketched in the opening paragraphs are but the more dramatic happenings in societies which are undergoing change at a more rapid rate than they have hitherto experienced. Furthermore the rate of change is most uneven as the urban centres begin to match in extravagance those of the western industrial nations, while the lot of the farmer seems scarcely to improve and the unskilled urban worker gazes at but cannot participate in the affluent living of the new élites. Again, these changes are taking place in a world in which the gap widens between the living standards of the richer and the poorer nations. The average *per capita* income in the United States is now double that of the nations of western Europe, between three and four times that of the U.S.S.R. and eastern European countries, and forty times that of India, most of the tropical African states and the poorer among the Latin American nations. But the disparity is not only between nations. Within both the United States and most of the poorer nations wealth is becoming less rather than more evenly distributed.

The study of the ongoing social processes in the poorer nations, the underdeveloped or developing countries as they are often termed, cannot be isolated from the examination of their relationship with the wealthy industrial nations. Conversely, of course, a study which neglects the processes internal to the poorer nations, treating them as pawns in the games of international politics and ascribing crises largely to external factors, is equally unrewarding. In the following pages I shall try to indicate the relationships between rich and poor nations, but my main concern will be with the internal processes of change in the latter.

This, of course, is a vast field in itself; each of the social sciences makes its own contribution and each writer is limited by the techniques of his own discipline. The viewpoints adopted by the sociologists themselves are varied in the extreme. Rather than try to evaluate their approaches (though I do criticize some of the modernization hypotheses in chapter 3) I intend to offer my own. In basing my analysis on the changing patterns of social stratification in the poorer nations I am being deliberately idiosyncratic and perhaps provocative.

In some, the term social stratification will evoke concepts of class, class consciousness and class conflict. To try to understand social processes in terms of class conflict – however one may define class – is quite legitimate; it is not however useful to expect that classes, as we understand them in western industrial society, will necessarily develop in the poorer developing nations. In fact a cursory study seems to indicate that the most violent conflicts are between ethnic and religious groups and not between socio-economic classes. Thus, while we may ultimately discard classes in one form or another, our primary purpose is to study society in terms of its stratification; in other words we are providing a framework of analysis rather than a description of institutions.

There are two aspects of stratification: the distribution of social inequality – the static aspect; and the relationship between those unequally placed in society – the dynamic aspect. Inequality among men is apparent in every society, even when it is based solely upon age. It is less easy to define precisely what it is that is so unevenly distributed and even harder to express these qualities in quantitative terms. And so social realities are apt to be obscured by arguments about concepts and measurement. Three qualities are usually cited – power, wealth and prestige; none of these is reducible in terms of the other two, yet they are obviously not unrelated. Of these, power is the most important. I would define it as the ability to impose one's will on the behaviour of others. Such power derives from the control of economic resources, from positions of authority (in the political sphere for instance) and from personal influence – which may in turn derive from belief in the legitimacy of the authority wielded, from wealth and from personal characteristics. A clear ranking in terms of power is obviously difficult inasmuch as exchanges between individuals occur in many different spheres and in each exchange the interpretation of the outcome by the individuals concerned may differ – each may think himself the winner. Nevertheless the distinction between weak and powerful is a valid one. Wealth concerns the rewards bestowed by society upon its members. We think we can measure it precisely in terms of cash income but the evaluation of immediate and future incomes and of non-monetary rewards raises problems; so too does the fact that each society will rank these types of rewards according to its own scale of values. The interrelationship between these two modes of ranking may be seen in a number of ways. Those with power will tend to seek the appropriate rewards; those whose wealth comes from the control of economic resources will tend to seek power in the political sphere in order to protect their economic interests. Elements of power and wealth are combined in the third mode of ranking – that of prestige; though it is possible, as in the case of religious or saintly men, to have high prestige without the exercise of power or the possession of material wealth. Prestige is manifest in the deference observable in inter-personal behaviour.

So far we have been specifying the qualities by which an

observer might describe inequality and the social ranking of individuals. Two other distributional aspects are important: firstly, the degree of mobility within the ranking systems – the rate and means by which lowly placed persons can move upwards and vice versa; secondly the degree to which people of similar rank interact as social equals forming recognizable social groups with distinctive styles of living and enjoying a consciousness of their identity which acts as a constraint to the membership of the upwardly or downwardly mobile. Such groups one might term status groups. Usually we take their existence for granted in our own industrial society, but they may be far less in evidence in the traditional societies of the poorer nations.

To understand the behaviour of members of any one society it is not our model of their social stratification (based upon our own preconceived ideas of what is significant) which is important, but theirs. Only in considering the outcomes of their behaviour should we investigate the correspondence between their models and our own, in the hope that our own model might prove more successful in prediction. Our own model might well display weaknesses in the definition of categories and in measurement. The members of a society will usually be found to hold a number of different models; any suggestion that there is a complete consensus in a society, as to its pattern of stratification and the values enshrined in this, is palpably false.

Individuals will perceive the stratification of their society according to their own position in the ranking and to their past experiences of mobility. They may operate inconsistent models, using one to describe the local community, another within the country as a whole. Implicit in the study of stratification is the assumption that every man is seeking to improve his own position, albeit at the expense of his neighbour; but as we shall see there are many who through their frustrations or through their acceptance of certain religious beliefs and ideologies (propagated perhaps by the wealthy and powerful) have sought alternative goals, and their perception of the stratification of their society is thereby affected.

The possible models can perhaps be best illustrated by outlining two contrasting variants. In the one, the pattern of inequality in society is seen to be legitimate and it is believed that positions of high rank are open to all; the emphasis is thus on personal achievement of these positions, relying heavily perhaps on the patronage of those already above oneself. In such a model, emphasis is placed on the functional interdependence of persons of different rank. In the other contrasting model the range of inequality in the society and/or the permitted means of attaining high rank are not accepted; a complete redistribution is sought; here the emphasis is on the co-operation of those similarly disadvantaged to attain their ends, with the corresponding co-operation of the privileged strata to preserve their interests. The conflict between these strata with diverse interests is stressed. Thus, boldly expressed, one would expect the highly ranked in society, the haves, to operate the functional model, and the lowly ranked, the have-nots, the conflict model. So neat an arrangement is rarely found in practice however. For we have to take into account the success of the highly ranked in propagating their own ideology, the persisting effect, in societies changing rapidly, of earlier models and of the importance of intra-class differences, within strata.

The actions of the individual member of society may, in the crudest manner, be interpreted in the sense of these models; he is either trying to achieve a higher rank for himself or to alter, in co-operation with others, the distribution of power, rewards and prestige. In the former case he will probably be seeking conformity between the different modes of ranking; thus for instance if he is powerful he will seek commensurate rewards and deference. When he is frustrated in his efforts to rise in rank – as he so often will be, for there are few, if any, societies in which the actual rates of social mobility exceed individual expectations – a number of responses are possible. He may continue to strive as before, hoping for success at some future date. He may stress the qualities which are not generally cited as criteria of stratification – for instance moral probity as in the case of the working-class man who says he is 'poor but honest'. He may compensate for a failure to rise on one mode of ranking by emphasizing another – the rich man who is denied power becomes extravagantly ostentatious. For the highly frustrated there are retreats into fantasy, as provided by some religious sects, in emigration to another society where the experienced constraints on mobility are believed to be non-existent, and in apathy often manifested in a general lack of concern for public affairs punctuated by sporadic outbreaks of unstructured violence.

We may speak of social class when members of a status group are conscious of their common interests with respect to the distribution of power and rewards in their society and seek in consequence either to improve their share or to prevent the dilution of their existing shares. Furthermore a social class is a relatively permanent group, though individuals are continually entering and leaving it, either through birth and death or through social mobility.

Within a society there may, empirically, be any number of social classes, reflecting slightly different interests. Inasmuch as one sees society in terms of opposed groups, there can ultimately be but two great classes. But as the classes are defined in increasingly broad terms so do the internal divisions within classes become more significant. These divisions may arise from differences in interest, such as occupation, or from different perceptions of the stratification system, with the attitudes of substantial groups corresponding to the individual responses to frustration cited above. Thus within a class will be those who continue to struggle to achieve their goals, those who seek alternative goals, and those who are apathetic. Furthermore class consciousness implies co-operation to attain shared goals and class ideology therefore has a strong egalitarian flavour; yet this is always countered by competition for power and rewards within the class and, perhaps, by the desire of some to move into the opposed class.

We may better appreciate these intra-class divisions in our later discussions of the urban wage labourer or the rural peasant. On occasion a working-class or peasant unity may be voiced; but at other times the internal divisions seem to be of overriding significance. Moreover the individual may use one model to describe stratification within his class – one stressing the achievement of a higher rank – and another, a conflict model, to describe the relationship between his own class and the other.

In this rather cursory and abstract discussion of social stratification I have tried to relate many of the themes which will dominate the succeeding chapters. As I shall explain later, I am sceptical of attempts to describe stages through which all societies pass by processes of unilinear evolution. If societies are ranked along a simple dimension according to some criterion of current development this is unlikely in fact to tell one much about their future prospects. Social change results from the continual interaction between individuals and groups seeking, through their use of existing resources and new opportunities, to improve their position in the social hierarchy. This I repeat is an idiosyncratic and perhaps a narrow interpretation of the social process. Its value lies, in part, in directing attention to, and stimulating further examination of, factors which are only too often neglected in the current sociological literature.

Inasmuch as one sees social change as the result of the interplay of a vast number of variables (the relative importance of which we are most unsure and whose values are often difficult, if not impossible, to measure), attempts at prediction for any single county or society are almost fruitless. How much less can one predict the future of the poorer nations in general? At best one can explain past changes through hindsight.

In the following chapters my task is, therefore, to set out those variables which I consider to be important. I shall illustrate my themes with examples taken from three areas: India; tropical Africa – especially Nigeria; and the north-western states of south America with their substantial Indian populations. I have selected these countries because of their very different cultural backgrounds; for I believe that the changes taking place in them can be analysed within the same conceptual framework. All are among the poorer nations of the world. The average *per-capita* income in India is £28 per annum; in tropical Africa it ranges from £18 in the poorer countries such as Upper Volta, through £29 for Nigeria and Tanzania to nearly £100 in Ghana and the Ivory Coast; incomes in the South American states range between £73 in Bolivia and £144 in Peru.

All the countries cited have experienced colonialism. The South American states did in fact gain their independence three quarters of a century before most societies of tropical Africa lost theirs. But this difference is contrasted with the relatively uniform manner in which all these countries have developed industrially in the present century, largely with foreign capital investment, and have in even more recent decades allowed political participation to the masses and vastly extended the basic social services, notably education.

Although I have tried to restrict the area from which I draw my examples I am conscious of the mental agility which I demand of the reader as I illustrate one theme with case material from one continent, the next theme from another. Let me, therefore, at this point briefly summarize the argument running through the following pages, linking my statements on the nature of social stratification to the content of individual chapters.

The societies discussed here are all undergoing social change at a rate more rapid than hitherto witnessed in the world – or at least some parts of them are, for the incidence of the western impact varies widely. Men and women are grasping at the new opportunities provided both to better their material conditions in absolute terms and also to improve their positions in the social ranking in their own societies. To achieve these goals they both exploit traditional and modern values, participate in traditionally- or modern-orientated associations. One can understand their actions only in terms of their own image of their social environment – the structure of their society, the constraints which it places on some actions, the sanctions of approval which it bestows on others. The individual's image of his society is, furthermore largely conditioned by the values which he has internalized in his upbringing and his own particular experiences. For the most part, the men whose activities are described in the following pages have been born into largely traditionally-orientated rural homes yet are now educated in the western idiom, and working in factories, mines or offices. We are dealing with a transitory state of affairs, for there is abundant evidence that those who have entered the modern sector of the economy not only intend that their children should in turn be engaged in it, but that their children should also attain positions of social rank equivalent to, or better than, those of their parents. Thus one sees the creation of almost hereditary categories; and on the rate of economic development will depend the future degree of mobility from the traditional into the modern sectors.

Our starting-point is the variety of traditional social structures in the poorer nations, which I illustrate with examples from a tribally organized Ibo village of Nigeria, a caste-structured village in southern India and a Peruvian village in the high Andes which one might loosely term feudal. I then comment upon the patterns of social stratification which prevail in these societies, for it is these concepts and values which the migrant brings with him to the town.

Next I outline the nature of the western impact on the poorer nations – a phenomenon well enough known to most readers. I would stress however, first, the nature of new opportunities provided – the growing of cash crops, wage labour in factory or office, positions of power and authority in the new political structures. Secondly, although the present level of economic development in these nations remains abysmally low, if measured in *per-capita* income rather than by the technology of isolated enterprises, yet the demands of the people for political representation and social services match those of the industrial nations. Many of the received theories describing the 'modernization' process in the poorer nations are both evolutionary and ethnocentric. Yet, as the material presented in these first two chapters shows, the poorer nations have no common starting-point, nor can their progress be equated with the patterns of development observed in the western industrial nations from the sixteenth to the nineteenth centuries. For while the latter grew by exploiting the wealth of the little known parts of the world, the poorer nations of today are heavily dependent upon the industrial nations. The theories of modernization current in the 1950s are today being challenged on two main fronts. Firstly, politically committed sociologists are attempting to describe the dependency of the poorer nations in the terms of their own discipline. Secondly, sociological theories which focused upon the institutions and values of a society, to the neglect of the individual (save that he accepted the values or was held to be a social deviant) are now being challenged by other approaches in which the individual, continually choosing between alternative courses of action, comes to the fore; interest is centred on the innovator, the entrepreneur (the deviant of earlier theories, now relieved of pejorative overtones). In explaining the ultimate action of the individual, we must take into account a number of variables.

This process of change can best be studied in the events of a small community. In chapter 5 I summarize at some length the excellent description of Scarlett Epstein of two neighbouring South Indian villages.[1] She not only demonstrates the nature of change in a rural area consequent upon the introduction of large-scale irrigation, but she teaches a most valuable lesson that change can take different forms depending upon the nature of the technological change – for while one village benefited directly from the irrigation, the other had to exploit subsidiary opportunities. Furthermore we see in each village which categories of people can and do take advantage of the new opportunities. In their so doing the traditional social ranking is disturbed and friction and protest results as the aspiring element of the society attempts to consolidate its new position while the threatened element tries to maintain its former prestige and authority. The village protests vividly described by Epstein formed no part of a wider organized movement, though they were undoubtedly repeated elsewhere. In looking at forms of general rural protest we must turn to other continents to note, for example, the cargo cults – a millennial movement of the Pacific Islands and the peasant movements of Latin America. In his own recent work Eric Wolf has spelled out the conditions under which rural protest becomes general and effective, emphasizing that those who revolt are not necessarily the poorest or the most exploited but those in whom the experience of change has bred most frustration.[2]

The rapid growth of the cities of the poorer nations is one of the most significant aspects of this development. Administrators struggle with problems of housing and sanitation; politicians fear the volatile outbursts of the poor and unemployed. Men leave their villages where they see little or no opportunity for them to use their initiative and education; they see the town as providing these opportunities – and so it does, but for far fewer than those who migrate. The choice of the migrant is constrained by his own wealth, or lack of it, his level of education, his personal contacts. Again, the choice is open, in theory, for the migrant to cast off much of his allegiance to his village and to espouse new urban values. In practice it is usually difficult for him to do so. Philip Mayer has described the rather startling dichotomy between the tradition-oriented 'red' Xhosa of East London, and the urban-oriented 'school' men.[3] Elsewhere the distinction is less sharp as men alternately manipulate traditional values and relationships and modern ones to achieve their goals. Yet a feature of many of these cities is the associations based upon primordial ties of village, ethnic group or caste through which men endeavour to adapt to, and prosper in, urban living. It is sometimes held that while traditional values may be upheld in the home of the city migrant, in the work situation values common to all industrial situations will prevail; but a study of a modern Indian factory suggests that even here relationships are still expressed largely in the traditional idiom. Too few studies have yet been made of the overall view which the city dweller has of the stratification pattern in which he is involved; but the retention of the traditional values of his society, his own experience of social mobility, the weakness of trade unions and the strength of primordial associations all frustrate the development of class consciousness as we understand that term. Yet even though protest movements may ostensibly develop amid criteria other than economic interest, we may still endeavour to interpret them in terms of economic and social frustration.

Poverty and unemployment dominate any description of the city migrant. But, for a few, usually men who have attained a high level of western education, posts in the political and economic sphere are open, which reward them with a style of life commensurate with that enjoyed by those similarly qualified in the industrial nations. These men, let us loosely call them the élite, virtually control their nations – though subject to the political and economic constraints of dependence upon the industrial nations. But these élite are not similarly recruited nor do they have similar economic interests; thus at one extreme are the South American oligarchies, heirs (socially if not strictly by descent) of the Spanish colonial rulers and dependent upon their landed estates; at the other extreme are the élites of the newly independent African nations, men who in many cases have risen in a single generation from the traditional village and whose political and economic control is exercised through their civil service post. Again these élites are far from homogeneous, for the criteria for the distribution of power, wealth and prestige are both varied and frequently not accepted by all. Thus although the members of the élite of an African nation tend to have a common social background and educational experience, rivalry for power occurs between politicians, civil servants, army officers, each stressing the legitimacy of those criteria – popular support, educational qualifications, force – which favours itself. By the nationally propagated ideologies – the three S's of Gandhi, *Négritude*, the populism of Latin America – the politically dominant section of the élite attempts both to induce cohesion within its own ranks and also to legitimate its dominant position in the sight of the masses. The political party is the instrument for securing the necessary popular support at elections.

In these chapters I have suggested a number of variables – the nature of rural demands and the form of rural protest; the poverty and unemployment in the cities, the image of the migrants of their society and the associations through which they pursue their goals; the characteristics of the dominant élite and the extent and nature of intra-élite competition for power. The outcome in any country is dependent upon these variables. In one country one finds stagnation, in another rapid change without marked violence, while in a third a revolutionary attempt is made to effect structural changes. These outcomes can be predicted only to the extent that we understand these variables and the relationship between them. Valid universal generalizations are certain to be too vague to have any useful meaning for us. The five examples – Nigeria, Colombia, Peru, Cuba and Tanzania – with which I end the book demonstrate the different outcomes and give a hint of the complexity of the variables outlined.

2   Traditional Societies

Peasant societies the world over have been said to exhibit a number of functionally related characteristics, which inhibit their social and economic development. The elements of this culture include the strong subordination of personal aims to those of the family and a high degree of mutual distrust and suspicion between members of different families, resulting in a low level of co-operative activity. It is believed by peasants that social benefits are limited and that the gain of one member of a community can only be at the expense of another. Peasants have limited aspirations, a limited view of the world and generally lack any sense of deferred gratification; they are unable to conceive the content of roles with which they are, as yet, unfamiliar. Peasants have a strong dependence on, yet hostility towards, government authority. They are fatalistic towards the world and lack the innovating spirit. These characteristics are, it would appear, the mirror opposite of those attributed to the idealized men of western industrial societies.

Substantiating examples of these traits are usually cited from peasant studies in Latin America and southern Europe and occasionally India. They would thus seem to refer to societies in which the peasant is involved in a market economy and in which the rural society of the peasant is contrasted with the urban society of the towns with their ruling literate aristocracies, the craftsmen and traders. Other definitions of peasants, however, emphasize their continued and substantial dependence upon subsistence agriculture. The characteristics listed in the above paragraph thus describe the rural population in all the poorer nations of the world – in Africa, Latin America and Asia.

Just as the impact of the industrial West on the communities of the poorer nations is so often seen in the most diffuse terms –

a 'wind of change' which gradually permeates the traditional society – so is it common to find that the differentiation within and between traditional societies is either subordinated to the examination of their common features or even neglected completely. Yet, I would argue, these differences are fundamental to the study of the changes which these societies are presently undergoing.

In the first place there is a fundamental difference in the patterns of social stratification in traditional societies. The range of variations is, of course, immense; but I would distinguish two ideal types – tribal and peasant societies. Tribal societies are essentially open, that is to say positions of power and wealth are open to all members of the society and are frequently achieved by men who have been born into humble homes; conversely the sons of the rich and powerful do not retain the status of their fathers. Such patterns of stratification are common in Africa both in societies with very low levels of political organization and in many of the complexly structured kingdoms where, although the monarchy is hereditary, senior chieftaincies may be open to all. In such societies the significant social units are often, though not always, defined in terms of descent. A peasant society, as I would like to define it is, in contrast, closed. That is, control of the offices of authority and of economic resources – land – is vested in a restricted category of persons – the aristocracy, a high-ranking caste, dominant ethnic group. The dominance of the superior group is maintained variously by their economic sanctions, their control of force and by a religious ideology which legitimizes their status. Peasant apathy is here the reflection of minimal amount of social mobility which is possible in such a society.

These two ideal types are not however mutually exclusive; for within the rural community of the peasant society a substantial degree of social mobility may be possible. Families may grow suddenly rich and influential and then decline again in the next generation. The peasant village *may* be tribally structured. Or, to return to the analytic framework suggested in the previous chapter, the peasant farmer may be operating with two models of stratification, one being used in a national context, the other in the local context. I shall return to this theme later in this chapter.

In studying the stratification pattern of traditional societies we are looking not merely at a static ranking of the distribution of power and rewards but at a process whereby individuals are seeking, either by competition or co-operation with others, to improve their own positions. This is a process which has been going on since the beginnings of human society. From a vantage-point within the traditional society we may see how the many and varied elements in the impact of the West – colonial rule, new religions, new consumer goods – are manipulated by individuals and groups to their own ends. Other scholars however would prefer to describe the western impact not in terms of competing individuals but of conflicting or incompatible values, arguing that those of western society are antithetical to those of traditional society and that their necessary acceptance, if the society is to develop, is impeded by the resistance of the traditional values. Two comments seem pertinent here. First, the significance of the traditional values is asserted; less often is it demonstrated that they are maintained when new opportunities make them obsolete. An anthropologist describing a south Italian village accepted that his peasant farmers displayed most of the characteristics listed in the opening paragraph of this chapter, yet many from this village had emigrated to the United States; could one honestly assert the absence of innovativeness and of risk-taking in such a community? Secondly, it is often asserted that western values are both favourable and necessary to development; traditional values are an impediment. This is, to say the least, highly debatable; just what *are* traditional values for instance – or western ones for that matter? I have already suggested the variation between traditional societies and the lack of consensus within many of them; just how far are specific traditional values incompatible with modern technology? Japanese industry is highly efficient notwithstanding its organization along lines reflecting traditional values of family and hierarchy which are quite unlike those of the western nations.

THREE VILLAGES

To illustrate the diversity of traditional societies let us look at three villages, one from each continent. The sketches given have been drawn from the much longer descriptions of social anthropologists who spent many months studying them. None of the three is, of course, typical of the continent; within each continent the variation is immense – from the small village polities in Africa to the mighty pre-colonial kingdoms; from the purely Indian communities of the Latin American states, still dependent on subsistence agriculture, albeit on land owned by a member of the white aristocracy, to the plantations employing Indians and persons of mixed blood and culture. None of the three is, however, unusual.

Agbaja (Southern Nigeria)[1]

Agbaja is a village group in the heart of the Ibo country in south-eastern Nigeria; it is termed a town by its people, though the compounds of individual households are scattered throughout the dense oil-palm bush. All the people of Agbaja trace descent from a pair of ancestors who were created by the high god and who lived, it is affirmed, where the central market now stands. These ancestors had eleven sons who, in turn, founded the eleven constituent villages of Agbaja, in one of which, Umueke, Margaret Green lived in the mid 1930s. Each village was in turn subdivided into wards and extended families on the basis of the accepted genealogy. Each of these units was generally territorially homogeneous; but ties of descent overrode those of residence. Agbaja recognized some ties with neighbouring village groups – its founding ancestor was said to have the same mother as the adjacent group. But the people of the whole village group linked by these ties never co-operated in any activity. In fact, there was little which brought together the members of Agbaja. Men and women from all the villages would come to the Agbaja market held every eight days; once a year they would come to the central shrines to serve their founding ancestors and common deities. And once a year the people cleared the paths from their own village to the central market – but they took care to arrive there at different times lest the mixture of excitement and inter-village rivalry should lead to fighting!

The most significant unit of social life was the village. Umueke had a population of approximately 360 engaged mainly in cultivating yams, cassava and maize with simple tools – hoes, axes and knives – and in expressing oil from the wild palms. The people lived in crude mud and thatch buildings. Land was held to be vested in the community which alone had the right to distribute it to members and alienate it to non-members; the individual could hold but a right to use an area, which was withdrawn as soon as he ceased to effectively cultivate the land. Because of the very high density of population in central Ibo-land, little land in Umueke was in fact seen as belonging to the entire village. Land tended to be partitioned down to the compound level and individuals were finding it increasingly difficult to gain land other than where their own fathers had farmed. Borrowing of land was becoming more frequent; but while the general principle of the inalienability of land was maintained, a wealthy individual could not accumulate land and become a powerful landlord. Wealth from farming came from hard work in cultivating the soil, and perhaps more pertinently, in having a large number of wives and sons whose surplus product could be used to enhance the prestige of the family. A large 'barn' (a series of racks) of stored yams was the usual mark of affluence. Wealth might also be achieved through trade.

The government of Umueke, if it could be so termed, rested with the council of family heads – men who held a staff of office handed down from father to eldest son (and perhaps intermediately by other sons). The staff holder, descended in the senior line from the eldest son of the village founder, was regarded as *primus inter pares*. But Miss Green describes how the incumbent of that office during her stay in the village was not a man of dominant personality and he seems to have been rather ineffective in village affairs. More impressive was another elder who happened to be the oldest man in the village. But meetings of the elders to discuss collective action and adjudicate disputes were usually held in the village square and anybody might attend. Young men and elders equally might speak for as long as they could command attention. Age and family office were thus qualities which might be exploited in the assertion of leadership, but they were not sufficient themselves. Similarly a wealthy farmer might give a big feast and assume a title but this gave him only increased prestige. The decisions of the elders, reached with the varying pressure of the younger men, could not be imposed by force for the village had no specialized police. Order was maintained, instead, through the rivalry between the villages and between their constituent parts. Thus communal activities were quickly completed because each segment sought to be first to finish its allotted task; market women of one segment spied on those of the other to ensure that they did not indulge in price cutting. The expulsion from the village of a man accused of a serious crime was carried out by all the young men.

This rivalry between the genealogical segments of the community extended beyond mere maintenance of order into the desire to enhance the prestige, power (through numerical superiority perhaps) or wealth of the segment. Thus the villages of Agbaja competed to have the school within their area – and, in a sense, they competed for Miss Green too. A man's standing within his group depended not so much on what he had achieved for himself as what he did for the group; a man who did not use his own position to benefit those of his extended family and village members would be despised. Thus, to give a much cited example, an educated man was expected to finance the schooling of his young relatives so that they too could reach his own new status.

Tanjore (Southern India)[2]

Very different is the Tamil-speaking village in the Tanjore District of South India studied by André Beteille. It is situated in a fertile plain, well irrigated for the past two thousand years. It was founded as a Brahmin settlement, presumably incorporating an indigenous population, too, at this early period and successively was subordinate to various dynasties which ruled the area until the colonial period. A family of the Marathas, the last dynasty, still lives in the village but it has lost most of the land which it had once owned.

Hindu religion recognizes four major castes (or varna) – the priests; warriors; traders; and farmers, artisans and craftsmen together with the outcastes. But the significant local groups are the jati, often termed sub-castes (though there may be more than one level of subdivision), recognized within a single village or neighbouring villages. The Tanjore village had a population of

1,400 in the mid 1960s – 340 of whom were Brahmins. 680 were of non-Brahmin castes (four fifths of them being of farming castes, the remainder of craft and service castes) and 370 were Adi-Dravidian or outcastes. Each of these three broad categories of villagers contained a number of proudly distinct and largely endogamous *jati*.

The Brahmins lived along a single street in well-designed and constructed houses. The Adi-Dravidians lived only a hundred yards away in poor mud and thatch houses, haphazardly sited but in a separate quarter. Between the two, intermediate both in location and style, were the houses of the non-Brahmins. Furthermore members of each *jati* tended to live together. The effects of residential segregation were enhanced by differences in dress and speech which reflected caste differences as well as wealth. Thus although the Brahmins usually spoke Tamil, they were well versed too in Sanskrit. The concepts of pollution limited the amount and type of social interaction between villagers. Thus, not only were there stringent rules governing the sharing of food between members of different *jati* but non-Brahmins and outcastes were not even allowed to enter the Brahmin street; similarly no Brahmin would enter the ward of the outcastes – he would have felt polluted were he to do so, while the outcastes would have seen the visit as bringing ill luck to them.

The social life of the Brahmins and Adi-Dravidians especially was in practice confined to their respective streets and ward. They settled their disputes for instance without reference to any village assembly. Yet the three caste categories in the village were economically interdependent, these relationships too being sanctioned by religion as a heaven-ordained system in which merit lay in fulfilling the role assigned to one, a reward for the meritorious being believed to be reincarnation into a higher caste. Broadly speaking, the Brahmins were the owners of the land and lived from its rents and from priestly and educational duties; the non-Brahmins were tenant farmers and the Adi-Dravidians were agricultural labourers, street-sweepers and the like. However, the current practice is not so idealized for there have been many sales of land, particularly by Brahmins who try to maintain their expected style of life or use the proceeds to acquire a western education for their children. The land has been bought by non-Brahmins and by men outside the village. Nevertheless three quarters of the village land is still owned by men who do not cultivate it, even though the largest holdings are now no more than twenty-five acres (many big landowners, however, register their land in the names of relatives and thus avoid its sequestration in the post-independence measures of land redistribution). Of the landowners resident in the village all were Brahmins. The tenant farmer was expected to give his landlord between two thirds and three quarters of his crop, even though he had provided the seed and the tools of cultivation; laws to reduce this proportion to 40 per cent have not been very effective. Today, therefore, economic categories (albeit hard to define exactly for a man may well own one plot, rent another) do not coincide exactly with caste divisions.

In the past the local government of the village rested almost exclusively with the Brahmins, being possessed of economic power and learning (they have dominated the local school since its opening in 1926). With elected councils the control of the *panchayat* has now passed to the numerically dominant non-Brahmins; the Brahmins tend to stand aloof from village affairs in order that they should not be seen to be defeated in a contest for power; the Adi-Dravidians are still too poor and too illiterate to make a significant contribution.

The caste system is often portrayed as one of rigid ascription. This is not strictly so. A man could not of course move from one caste to another; but although the ritual relationships between *jati* were agreed by those concerned, the overall ranking of *jati* was not necessarily a subject of consensus. Members of a *jati* could adopt the styles of living of higher groups, increasing their sanskritization and hoping thus to gain recognition for their aspired status. Within a village this might take several generations; a group migrating from one village to another could rise more quickly. Today, as has been shown above, wealth through landowning and participation in political parties and elected councils do not depend exclusively on caste membership and so form alternative routes to power. Between the leading Brahmins and the newly rich landlords and political leaders of this Tanjore village there was considerable rivalry.

Vicos (Peru)[3]

Yet another contrast is provided by Vicos, a village in the high Andes of Peru which was both studied by Alan Holmberg and his pupils and subsequently completely changed by them in a programme of community development. Remains of the ancient Inca civilization are still visible and a third of Peru's nine million people are identified as Indians. Of these Indians one third now live on the vast landed estates set up by the Spaniards, one third live on small independent farms and a third have left the land to work in the mines. The changes which have been effected on the Peruvian coast have been slow to penetrate the highland valleys where the communities remain in substantial isolation; local dialect differences are still obstacles to communication. The area is over-populated and lacking in capital for development. Poverty and isolation have, it is alleged, made the Indian distrustful of the outside world and resistant to integration with it.

Vicos itself is 250 miles from Lima, the Peruvian capital, its 55 square miles lying between 9,000 and 14,000 feet above sea-level. Its cultivated land grows maize, potatoes, barley and wheat; grazing land supports cattle and sheep. The village estate was until the 1950s owned by the state but was leased every ten years to the highest bidder in public auction. Ten per cent of the land was held by this lessee or patron for cultivating for commercial purposes; the remaining 90 per cent was held by over three hundred Indian families. Each Indian family was required to supply the labour of one adult male for three days each week to work on the patron's land; in addition the Indians could be called upon to supply animals whenever the patron needed them and domestic services for his household.

Work on the patron's land was supervised by six foremen, Indians who were selected by the patron. These were elderly men who also held a high position in the community. Not only did they organize the labour force on the patron's land but they generally settled disputes in the village. The patron was, in effect, not unlike a feudal baron controlling most aspects of the life of his tenants through his power to confiscate tools and land for misdemeanours. He was little interested in the progress of his village; for by 1950 only five persons in the village could read and write, the local school being so poor as to be distrusted by the Indians. The only sphere over which the patron had little control was that of religion. Here the village priest was supreme and locally elected mayors organized the main festivals. (While this office gave them prestige, but not secular power, it was a stepping-stone to selection as a foreman.)

Descriptions of the estates often concentrate upon the relationship of inequality between the patron and his Indians. Less frequently do they describe the differences within the Indian population. In Vicos, the villagers identified three categories: the rich, numbering a sixth of all families; the middle group numbering nearly two fifths; and the poor. The division was based upon styles of living but the principal criterion of definition used was wealth. The acquisition of wealth seems to have resulted from hard work and ability. The rich farmed well, lent and spent money judiciously and accumulated a herd of several cattle and other livestock. Their wealth, however, could be just as quickly lost through the accidents of sickness and disease; at their death their property was divided among their several children so that the shares of each were often small. There seems therefore to have been a high rate of social mobility within the Indian community. Locally, this mobility was generally attributed to one's personal luck.

The inequalities within Vicos society resulted in a number of relationships of dependence between the rich and the poor. The poor tended to describe the rich as misers while the rich looked upon the poor as thieves. The rich Indians sought to enter into relationships with the socially superior *mestizos*; the middle group of Indians emulated the rich. A study of everyday events in Vicos would certainly have illustrated the competition between villagers for rank.

TRIBAL AND PEASANT STRATIFICATION

In each of these three societies, as in fact in all tribal and peasant societies, there is an uneven distribution of power and rewards. The difference between the style of life of the rich Brahmin and the depressed outcaste, the landlord and the Indian peasant, are quite clear to the external observer. Less patent, perhaps, are the

33

differences within an African society with a low level of technology. To the untrained observer house styles look alike and in the large rambling compounds the number of wives held by each man is not easily discovered. But to the member of such a society the difference between the affluence and prestige of the farmer with a large barn of yams and the poor farmer subsisting on a diet of cassava is real enough.

However, tribal and peasant societies must be clearly distinguished on two counts. In the former positions of authority and wealth are open to all, or at least to most, of the members of the society. In the latter it is impossible for a man to suddenly change his caste and very difficult for a caste to raise itself in the social hierarchy; there is little opportunity too for the Peruvian peasant to enter the ranks of the local and national aristocracy. Peasant society is thus closed. Furthermore, in the tribal society the product of a man's labour is largely his own, though he may have to support elderly kin and pay a relatively light tribute to his chief. The differences in wealth thus depend largely on the degree of effort expended, on skill for instance, in assesssing soil types and on luck with the weather. In the peasant societies a man owes a large product of his labour to his landlord, a member of the dominant group, in return for the right to use the land. Yet these obligations fall on all peasants and among them one will find differences in wealth, based, as in the tribal society, on effort, skills and luck.

Let us look again at the structure of a tribal society – here a highly idealized one. Its most important characteristic is usually that the basic social divisions are not between horizontal strata, defined in terms of wealth and power but vertical divisions into descent groups defined in genealogical terms. Each descent group is similarly structured and, in particular, each will have its own position of authority, its wealthy and poor members. Yet complete equality between the descent groups over time is not possible. Members of one will acquire more wives than those of another; they will have more children and thus need more land – land which can be gained only at the expense of a neighbouring group. One may, therefore, view the process of village life in terms of continuing competition between descent groups for women and for land, and indirectly for that corporate prestige which will make their men more desired as husbands and increase their power in the tribunals which adjudicate claims to land. In theory one descent group might outstrip all of its rivals; but there are institutionalized processes which tend to prevent this, for effective competition demands an approximate equality between competitors. Fission may occur in the larger groups, splitting them into smaller autonomous units; fusion may occur between the smallest units. In Umueke, a balance was maintained by detaching a segment of one large descent group and adding it, for practical purposes as in path clearing, to another group. In time one suspects the genealogies would be altered so as to describe accurately the social divisions locally recognized.

While one emphasizes the competition between descent groups, one must also note the bonds between them. Each group is an exogamous unit – its men must seek wives from other groups. Again, age groups are an important feature of village life, especially for the younger men (in some Ibo villages for the older ones too – the senior age grade constituting the village council). Thus in many an inter-descent group contest individual men will find that among their adversaries are their in-laws and age mates, and though their loyalty to their descent group might remain paramount, the degree to which they can press their claims will be moderated. Again on one occasion rival descent groups oppose each other; on the next they will be allied as their village collectively opposes its neighbour.

What is the role of the individual in this competitive process? In the first place he seeks his own personal gain. He strives to become wealthy; he seeks power over his fellows. The rewards are for his personal enjoyment – he has a richer diet, he does not share his wives with his brothers; leisure from the tedium of farming is not only pleasant in itself but enables him to play a more active role in village politics. Corporate holding of land must never be confused with a communistic mode of living in which the product of each man is pooled for equal distribution to all. But the success of the individual benefits his descent group indirectly; he is expected to be generous – and his close kin will stand to gain most; he is expected to use his resources to enhance the status of the whole group. Thus, if it were involved in a land dispute he would be expected to support the litigation financially and use his influence to win a favourable decision. The successful man who refuses to aid and to lead the members of his descent group (and ultimately the whole village) is despised.

As we have noted already, success derives largely from skill, hard work and luck. With land, the basic resource, corporately owned, every man can obtain sufficient for his needs. And trading, a means of attaining considerable wealth, is open to all. But success may depend to a high degree on the support of one's fellows. The generous and popular farmer will get his friends to work on his farm at peak periods of activity; the trader will depend heavily on his reputation, for most of his dealings with his customers will be face to face. The miser will get no help on his farms, his customers will desert him. In many tribal societies chiefs are elected by and from among members of their descent groups; in others the selection is made by the ruler and existing chiefs but they will base their decisions to a substantial degree on the personal following of the respective candidates.

A position of wealth or power, once attained, does not pass to a man's heir. He cannot translate his farming or trading profits into personal control over land; in Africa he acquires wives and thus has many children. These are a source of prestige during his lifetime and will ensure that his praises are sung long after his death. But the laws of inheritance frequently provide for an equal distribution of the estate among (usually male) children or for division into as many equal parts as a man has wives who have borne sons. The shares of each child are thus minimal and cannot, without exercise of effort and skill considerable quickly bring wealth commensurate with that of the father. In fact in some tribal societies it is commonly said that the son of a rich father is disadvantaged as he does not have to struggle in his youth and so never learns how to work hard. It is significant that in such societies the richest men have usually risen from very humble homes. Similarly chiefly offices may be rotated through the segments of the descent group, and while the exact order of rotation may be sometimes overruled by other principles, it may be held most strongly that a man should not be succeeded directly by his own son. Every man in the group is thus eligible for the title and may be a candidate at some time during his adult life.

In a tribal society, such as the one outlined above, one would expect to find considerable stress placed upon two values: the desirability of power and wealth and the importance of the good opinion of one's fellows. The latter is to be gained in using success not only for one's personal benefit but also for that of the group. The source of achievement orientation stressed here is very different from that attributed to the protestant ascetic – a man who sees himself judged only by God and his own conscience.

Much as people in a tribal society admire the successful and generous man they are nevertheless jealous of him – his success could have been theirs too. Inequalities in society are seen therefore as deriving from fate and witchcraft. A common belief is that a man receives his 'fate' on being born into the world. This would seem to suggest a predestination which could only result in apathy; however there are means by which an individual can ameliorate or even worsen his fate. 'My fate is against me' is the common plea of the unsuccessful. In many societies it is believed that a man who suddenly and rather inexplicably (in the eyes of his fellows) achieves great wealth or power has used supernatural means and that these have often been directed against those nearest to him. A wealthy Yoruba trader might be said to have caused the death of his eldest child or the barrenness of a wife. The Tiv, also of Nigeria, see power as a form of witchcraft-potential. One man can rise in society only at the expense of his fellows. However this does not seem to deter men from trying to improve their position in their society; those who are less prosperous may try on occasion to devaluate the success of those who have surpassed them, but they are nevertheless grateful for the benefits which the successful man can bestow on his descent group and its individual members.

The Ibo have migrated to all parts of Nigeria as artisans, clerks and petty traders. The popular stereotype of the Ibo is of an achievement oriented, aggressive individual who does not disdain hard manual work. This is seen as the cause of their success outside their home areas. The few psychological tests which have been conducted seem to support this image of the Ibo. It is easy to relate this type of personality to the features of Ibo social structure outlined above, but there are dangers in attributing the dominance attained by the Ibo in the economic and political life of Nigeria, solely to the values held by them. Missions and schooling came relatively early to Ibo country, and although the speed with which they accepted western education is an indication of their competitive spirit, they did gain an advantage over peoples who had been denied the benefits of such education – such as the Hausa of the northern emirates, where the colonial administration had forbidden missionary activity in an attempt to maintain the strength of Islam and the political system which it supported. More significantly, the Ibo migrants overwhelmingly come from the most densely populated areas. The chances of obtaining sufficient land for farming are rapidly declining. The degree to which a man is willing to undertake menial tasks and the amount of effort and ingenuity employed in the town can be seen not as related exclusively to a value system but equally to the lack of alternative opportunities available at home.

To the extent that a high degree of social mobility may be possible within a rural peasant society, it may display many of the characteristics of the tribal society just described. But overriding any similarities is the fact that the peasant society is essentially closed, divided between one group which monopolizes the positions of power and great rewards and another which is permanently deprived of them. These closed groups are opposed to each other inasmuch as the dominant group seeks to preserve its privileged position while the disadvantaged groups would seek a more egalitarian society. But neither of the possible recourses to the latter in such a situation is effectively available. Individuals cannot – or can but infrequently – hope to enter the dominant group and thus share in its privileges. Both the resources of the underprivileged, and the sanctions available to the dominant group, are generally such that action to effect a redistribution of power and rewards in society is unlikely to succeed, short of a radical change in the social, political or economic environment of the community.

The efforts of the peasant tend to be directed towards enhancing his status, *vis-à-vis* his fellow men within his own community, and in attempting to ameliorate the exactions demanded by the dominant group – his landlord or political overlord in particular – to enter into a dependent relationship as a client of a member of the dominant group – his patron. These efforts may be further supported by religious beliefs which explain that inequality in power and wealth is of divine ordinance, that the individual should seek to fulfil the obligations attaching to the status into which he was born and that the rewards for fulfilment lie in a future life – in heaven for Christians, in a reincarnation for Hindus. Such beliefs, however, would seem to be more effective in maintaining the divisions between the closed groups in the society than in hindering social mobility within them.

In peasant societies land is allocated, ultimately, not by a corporate group of which the farmer is a member, but by a landlord. A man's descendants, in perpetuity, may continue to cultivate the same area of land; but individual holding is much more usual. A man's land will be divided equally between his sons; if the shares so received are insufficient to maintain a household, the sons must buy from those more favourably placed. In the peasant societies of Asia and Latin America men are usually monogamous; but a rich farmer who has several sons may leave each with less land than a moderately prosperous man leaves his sole heir. On the one hand a successful man can acquire land and so substantially transmit his status to his heirs; but on the other, inasmuch as land is subject to the processes of inheritance, differences in human fertility can lead some families to rise in status, others to fall.

Patronage and individual land-holding inevitably reduce the strength of corporate descent groups: in many peasant societies they are not significant social groups; the basic unit is the household (caste provides, in India, a focus for co-operation absent elsewhere). Differences in wealth here tend to be magnified for many of the poorest households are, as in Vicos, those of the aged (especially with only one spouse living) or the infirm – categories which tend to be less noticeable in the compound life of tribal Africa. Thus, a man who becomes a successful farmer or trader is not seen as benefiting a larger group; inasmuch as he can help others it tends to be through relationship of patronage, emphasizing the dependence of the recipient rather than his equality as a group member.

The successful peasant may not be able to enter the ranks of the dominant group, but he may well attempt to emulate their styles of living and so set himself apart from his fellows. In seeking power within his community he may aspire to and attain an office in the gift of the local landlord, or of the state; he will be judged by his fellows to have deserted their interests to further his own; he becomes the agent of the dominant group rather than the leader of the peasants.

These factors seem likely to provide at least a partial explanation of the characteristics of peasant society cited at the beginning of this chapter. In peasant, as in tribal, society men feel that they are, in a very general way, equal in moral worth. But in peasant society they have common interests in opposition to the dominant group which enhances their solidarity. This equality is thus in more marked contrast with the patently uneven distribution of wealth within peasant society. The outcome is the social isolation of the individual family and the intensity of competition between families. Co-operation is minimal. Gossip and scandal are rife as individuals seek to demonstrate that others who rank above them in wealth are less worthy in moral terms. Equality is asserted by the manipulation of several scales of ranking so that those who rank high on one scale, are placed low on another – and so everyone comes out with the same average score. The idea of the 'limited good' seems to reflect not a belief that the quantum of material goods cannot be increased but a rationalization that sudden increases are not likely and that gains can be achieved only at the expense of others – the social ranking is altered. Inasmuch as the villagers are suspicious of his wealth and influence, the successful man fears perhaps that to assume leadership thus would deprive him of much of the support necessary to maintain his prosperity; this would certainly be so if he were to be seen as defecting to the dominant group.

In delineating contrasting types, one is drawn to describe extreme cases. Not all tribal societies are so perfectly modelled on descent groups as the Ibo; not all peasant societies share the characteristics cited here. But in distinguishing these two types I have suggested a number of variables which determine the values, relative to the justification and distribution of inequality, which are found in traditional societies.

One question remains: how far do these values affect the rate of development? In much of the literature their importance seems to be overrated. Ibo achievement orientation is now stressed as a factor in determining their role in the Nigerian state. But, as far as we can tell, Ibo society was not rapidly changing in the pre-colonial centuries. The level of technology of traditional societies was so low that few improvements could have been developed internally. The members of these societies generally knew little about lands ten miles beyond their own villages and so received little stimulus from other cultures. Inasmuch as the individual was so dependent upon other members of his village innovations which threatened these relationships would seem, in social if not in purely economic terms, to be too costly. Each of these factors militates against the rapid development of social structure. Today new opportunities have been introduced externally and the members of some societies have been quick to exploit them. But so often we do not evaluate the attitudes of the members of the recipient society with the rewards offered. How far does the avid acceptance of a new technique depend on the values shared by the society or the perceived benefits of the innovation to individuals? Conversely, we are prone to ascribe to the society which is not progressing today, a lack of achievement orientation; but has it been offered the opportunities which have benefited its neighbours? Attitudes towards change should be studied not generally but in specific contexts, and in terms of actors' perceptions of their own advantage rather than of the values of their society.

Values relating to achievement may perhaps facilitate change in some cases; their relative absence may impede it in others – though their effect would seem to be short-lived if the changes bring economic rewards. Of perhaps greater significance are the social skills which accompany the varying patterns of stratification. Much of the success of the Ibo abroad (and of the ill feeling of the Nigerians towards them) derives from their group solidarity; men will endeavour to ensure that vacancies in their workplace are filled by relatives. In other societies the dominant skill is the manipulation of the patron–client relationship and there seems to be no reason why this should not prove useful in other situations. In one society, the good opinion of one's neighbours may be a necessary qualification, in another it is irrelevant. Finally, I have tended to assume that all the members of a society share common values and a modal personality type; this of course is not so. Men who seem ill-fitted to prosper in the traditional society may be just the ones to succeed with new opportunities.

3 The Impact of the West

The poorer nations are frequently described collectively as the
'third world', being distinguished thereby from the first or
western industrialized world and the second world of the Communist nations. The term seems to imply an independence from
either of the other two worlds and a degree of internal cohesion.
The leaders of the poorer nations do indeed often profess policies of non-alignment and attempt on occasion to exploit western–
communist rivalry. Yet though they may be united in this
feeling, as underprivileged societies, in practice they are not able
to pursue common policies. Were they to do so they would
clearly dominate the United Nations where they constitute two
thirds of the total membership.

In fact the poorer nations of the world are not independent in
any but a legalistic sense. They are as much a part of the western
industrial society as are the lower classes of the industrial
nations. That is to say, just as one has social stratification within
nations, so can one describe a pattern of stratification across
nations. The lower strata in both rich and poor countries may
differ greatly in culture, but at the apex of the poorer nations are
men and women who, to an ever-increasing degree, share, with
those of the rich nations, a common cultural heritage and style of
life – one might term it 'western', though 'international' would
probably be a more accurate designation today.

ECONOMIC DEPENDENCY

When the countries of western Europe began their mercantilist
development they took from the tropical countries precious
metals, spices and exotic luxuries for the use of their ruling
groups. Patterns of political domination varied considerably. The

43

impact of the West often did not reach the villages, save that one tax-collector was perhaps substituted for another; the indigenous cultures continued to persist. But from the mid nineteenth century the West increasingly sought not luxuries but the basic raw materials for its new industries – oil, iron, copper – or for commodities of mass consumption – coffee, cocoa, tea. The pattern of present economic domination is far more uniform than the pre-existing diversities.

In the north-west of South America the Spanish Conquistadores demolished the Inca empire – an empire that was large in extent and had a complex system of government though it was based upon a very simple technology. Estates were granted to the conquerors and they exploited the surplus labour of the Indian peasants, as described in the previous chapter; in coastal localities where sugar could be grown, they established plantations worked by slave labour. The Spanish (as did other European peoples elsewhere in Latin America) developed their own urban culture; the absentee landowners lived in the towns – and every wealthy family, as well as the professional people, businessmen and craftsmen, based their claim to high status on the possession of an estate. In the more remote areas the Indians maintained their cultural identity; elsewhere, through intermarriage with the Europeans and through cultural assimilation a *mestizo* population was created – a population defined in terms of cultural rather than of biological traits and sharply distinguished from the Indians on the one hand and the exclusive aristocracy on the other. At the beginning of the nineteenth century the local resident aristocracy successfully revolted against metropolitan rule and the several states extant today came into being. Independence does not seem to have stimulated economic development; the rewards which had formerly passed to Spain now flowed into local pockets but for consumption rather than for investment; rival factions within the aristocracies fought to control their distribution.

The great civilizations of India go back two or more millennia to the Aryan conquests which extended across the subcontinent between 1500 BC and AD 200. Over the succeeding centuries, dynasties rose and fell but the successive empires were powerful and highly organized. Lavish royal courts in the capital cities, large standing armies and well-developed bureau-cracies were characteristic. The land was appropriated by the rulers and the peasant farmer was taxed by a variety of systems. The British conquest of India spanned the last half of the eight-eenth and the first half of the nineteenth centuries. The jurisdic-tion of the East India Company eventually passed to the Crown; but while many areas were ruled directly by British civil servants, in others the traditional rulers maintained their own administra-tions with British support, guidance and ultimate control. Methods of tax-collection were adapted and reformed but the lot of the peasant was not materially altered.

Portuguese explorers reached the West African kingdom of Benin before Columbus set foot in the Americas; but European penetration of tropical Africa was slow and it remained, for three centuries, the 'Dark Continent'. The Portuguese and their suc-cessors did establish trading-posts in the interior of their terri-tories of Angola and Mozambique; but in West Africa trading was largely conducted from coastal forts or hulks. Slaves for shipment to the Americas were the main export and the supply was organized by the African peoples themselves. Some areas became denuded of population; but many of the larger king-doms which developed in these centuries owe their growth and success to the new opportunities provided by the slave trade. Yet, locally powerful though some of these kingdoms were, none attained the scale of the Indian or Inca empires. Over vast areas of Africa societies remained tribally structured and even many of the kingdoms were substantially egalitarian, the principal exceptions being the West African states conquered by the Fulani in the early part of the nineteenth century and the Bantu states of East Africa with their pastoralist rulers – notably Bunyoro, Ankole, Rwanda and Burundi. Political control of the interior of Africa passed to the European metropolitan powers in the 'scramble' of the 1880s when they mapped out their re-spective spheres; but local administration was not achieved in many areas until the 1920s. The British colonial administrators tended, in areas not subject to white settlement, to rule through the indigenous office holders, thus preserving the power of the traditional political structures. The French overtly favoured a more direct form of administration. But the difference between these contrasting forms of administration was more apparent than real. Common to both was an extreme paucity of officials and the consequent emphasis simply on the maintenance of law and order rather than on policies directed towards creating rapid economic development, development which might produce social dislocation.

The South American republics gained their independence in the first decades of the nineteenth century; India achieved hers in 1946, so stimulating the demands of nationalist leaders in other colonial territories, that by the end of 1960 most of Africa too had become independent. But political status seems to have had relatively little effect on the form and timing of the recent economic development of the poorer nations. Thus the industrialization of India proceeded simultaneously with that of the South American states. Of the African states which maintained their independence throughout the nineteenth century Liberia is very firmly economically tied to the United States and Ethiopia is among the poorest. In South Asia, Thailand seems to have gained little advantage over her neighbours in evading colonial domination.

The two most dominant features of recent economic development are the colossal scale of the foreign financed extractive industries, relative to the size and wealth of the poorer nations and the continuous backwardness of agricultural production. Let us examine more closely these, and other related themes.

Throughout vast areas of tropical Africa, Asia and Latin America, farmers continue to cultivate the land substantially in the same manner as their forefathers. The only difference, in some areas, is that they have less land to work as a result of the rapidly rising population. This stagnation of agriculture results from a variety of factors – ignorance, lack of capital, and a variety of social constraints which hinder the would-be innovator. However, it is often argued that, given his resources, the farmer is working efficiently. Too little research examines the improvements which a farmer might make, with acceptable levels of risk, within his own mode of farming. Too many schemes attempt to devise ideal systems of agriculture in which the existing patterns are completely destroyed. These usually require vast sums of capital expenditure, and, where farmers have to be displaced, may need a degree of coercion which can rarely be applied; an example of such coercion is the resettlement of the Kikuyu of Kenya after the Mau-Mau emergency. The relatively successful cotton-growing Gezeira scheme in the Sudan contrasts with the ill-fated attempts to grow groundnuts on mechanized estates in Tanganyika.

Some crops, destined for export, have been grown by farmers within their traditional agricultural system. Cocoa, coffee, cotton and groundnuts are grown in this manner throughout West Africa where the colonial governments, and especially the British, prohibited white settlement and the development of plantations. The cash income which reaches the farmers has promoted the development of the local economy, providing some new opportunities in crafts and trade. Yet, inasmuch as land becomes a more highly valued resource, the traditional descent groups are, as among the Yoruba of south-west Nigeria, correspondingly strengthened. The example described at length in a following chapter will demonstrate that the effect of innovations in breaking down traditional social structure depends on their specific character.

Elsewhere the major export crops are grown on estates financed by foreign capital and with the labour of men and women who have left their traditional communities. Examples are the sugar plantations of Latin America established in the sixteenth and succeeding centuries often with slave labour from Africa; the tea plantations of India established from the mid nineteenth century; the oil-palm estates of Unilever in the ex-Belgian Congo developed at the beginning of this century. Within Latin America there is today a contrast between the older types of monocultural estates in which a labour force of only a hundred workers still looks upon the owner as their patron, and the much larger and more recently developed estate, usually highly mechanized, whose workers may aptly be termed a rural proletariat. In general, the landlords of India and South America have done little or nothing to promote an agricultural revolution. In many descriptions of village India one reads that the landowners have been selling plots in order to maintain their traditional style of life; they have not rationalized their use of the land. In Latin America the traditional source of income still seems sufficient to

give the landowner a high social status and political influence and
to provide little incentive to increase the productivity of labour
or land.

In contrast to the continuing primitiveness of agriculture is
the advanced technology used in the mining industries. These
tend to be owned by some of the largest business corporations in
the world. The extraction of this wealth is relatively recent; tin-
mining was developed in Bolivia in the 1900s; Shell-B.P. were
exploring for oil in the Niger Delta for twenty years before the
fuel was finally discovered and production began in the early
1960s; the copper mines of Zambia date from the 1930s. These
industries tend to employ many of the most highly skilled and
hence the best paid workers in the state. By their very size they
virtually dominate the small states of Africa and Latin America.
Thus the capital invested in the Limba iron mine of Sierra
Leone was in 1961 equivalent to one sixth of the value of the
exports from *all* the West African states. Furthermore, the small
states find their export trade dominated by a single commodity,
the world demand and price for which can fluctuate violently.
Thus tin accounts for three quarters of Bolivia's exports, copper
for almost all of those of Zambia. The economy of other countries
is equally dominated by their reliance upon a single agricultural commodity – Colombia for instance is almost completely
dependent upon coffee. The situation is only marginally bettered
in the larger countries; thus one half of the exports both of
Nigeria and India come from three commodities. The relationship between the firms owning these industries and the governments of the host states is one of the major political issues of
these poorer nations, for only the largest and most affluent of the
poorer nations has an annual revenue which approaches that of
some of the huge, multinational corporations.

The industrializing nations of the west needed not only raw
materials for their factories but also a market for their products.
As a result the indigenous commerce and crafts of the tropical
world were often destroyed by foreign competition. In India for
instance the local textile industry collapsed at the beginning of
the nineteenth century although a new textile industry, financed
by British and some Indian capital was started in the 1850s.
Local crafts, too, declined as they could not compete with British

machine-made equivalents. In Lagos, Nigeria, a number of African businessmen were competing quite successfully with expatriate firms at the beginning of the century; but the latter gradually amalgamated and forced the former into decline. One company, the United Africa Company, a Unilever subsidiary, accounted in the 1950s for one third of Nigeria's imports and two fifths of her non-mineral exports. Nevertheless, although the indigenous independent businessman was forced out, the expatriate companies did provide training for a large number of agents, some of whom subsequently started operations on their own. In general, the economy of the poorer nations was distorted. A heavy investment of capital and labour in transport and construction to provide the infrastructure necessary for the exporting industries was balanced by the underdevelopment of manufacturing industries. The manufacturing industries currently being financed by western capital tend to be capital intensive and of a high technological standard; this seems necessary to assure the required profit margins. But the internal markets provided by the poorer nations are too meagre to provide many opportunities for industrial development – the populations of these countries being small and poverty-stricken. Planning on a continental scale is hampered when each state wishes to maximize its own industry, and raises tariffs against imports from neighbours, when each is equally suited to develop the manufacture of a given commodity and when communications between the states are so poor. The railways of colonial Africa, for instance, run inland from the coast, each tapping its own little hinterland. India, by virtue of her size has, in fact, been able to develop a sizeable manufacturing industry in which indigenous business families – the Tatas who own one of the world's biggest steel works, and the Birlas, Dalmias and Jains being well-known examples – have played a prominent part. Thus 17 per cent of India's gross domestic product comes from manufacturing, almost the same proportion as in Peru, though the *per-capita* income of the latter is double that of the former. (Compare the proportion in the industrial countries – over 30 per cent.) The development of manufacturing industry is least in tropical Africa where it accounts everywhere (except Kenya) for less than 5 per cent of the gross domestic product; in Nigeria, in spite of the recent growth of new factories around Lagos it is only 1 per cent. In Ghana the attempts by the Nkrumah government to promote and establish industries in default of private enterprise were most unhappy. Nevertheless, manufacturing is the most rapidly expanding sector of the economy of most of the poorer nations, being financed both by local and expatriate capital. But though this contributes to the increasing wealth of these countries, it does not necessarily reduce their dependence upon the industrialized West.

Let us briefly recapitulate the main features of the economy of the poorer nations. Production in the modern sector is dominated by a few commodities produced for export to the industrial nations. Most of the trade is in fact with these countries. Half of Colombia's trade is with the U.S.A., and a fifth with Europe and only 5 per cent with other Latin American countries – a pattern which is substantially replicated in neighbouring countries. The trade of African states is dominated by the erstwhile metropolitan country; in West African states less than 5 per cent of the trade is with their neighbours. The financing of plantation agriculture, of extractive and of much manufacturing industry has come from the industrial nations – largely from the U.S.A. in respect of South America and from the metropolitan countries in respect of the African colonies and India. Without this investment there could never have been development on this scale. Yet it is calculated by some that the annual outflow of the poorer nations in the form of interest on capital and loans, repatriated profits and the like, now exceeds the inflow of new investments and aid. To the extent that further economic development depends on the rate of saving within the country the limiting factors will continue to be the poverty of the masses, the reluctance of the wealthy to be taxed and the failure of expatriate-owned firms to retain their profits within the country of origin. Our task here, however, is not to provide solutions to the problems of economic development but to indicate the changes in the social structures that such development has already effected in the poorer nations.

Over vast areas – where development has been minimal and where export crops are grown by small farmers, alongside their subsistence foods – the traditional patterns of social structure have been maintained to a high degree. On the other hand a large number of people have been drawn into wage-earning. The proportions of the population vary widely from one country to another depending upon the character of the major commodities produced. Thus only 5 per cent of Nigeria's male labour force is wage-earning, while nearly 50 per cent of Zambia's is. The territorial distribution of plantation workers and miners is of course determined by the resources. But the employment of those engaged in manufacturing and tertiary industries and services tends to be in a few major centres, predominant among which are the national capitals. These are now growing at a rate disproportionate to other centres. Abidjan, capital of the Ivory Coast, and Accra, capital of Ghana, both accommodate 5 per cent of their respective countries' population. Almost all African towns are of recent creation and their growth has been accordingly rapid; Accra, for example, grew from 20,000 in 1914 to 135,000 in 1948 and 320,000 in 1960. In Peru the recent annual growth rate of the capital Lima, 4.4 per cent, has been almost double that of the provincial towns of the mountain areas. Indian towns too have grown – Bombay fivefold between 1901 and 1967 when its population exceeded four million, Poona nearly fourfold and Hyderabad by two and a half times over the same period, though much of this can be attributed not to immigration but to natural increase. These cities however are not only centres of employment, but also of unemployment, as the rate of migration to them increasingly exceeds the available opportunities. It is in the cities therefore that the disparity of wealth between rich and poor is greatest.

The uneven impact of economic development is not only seen in the growing disparity in wealth between the towns and their rural hinterlands but also between neighbouring regions and states. One region is blessed with mineral wealth or soils suitable for export crops while its neighbour is barren. Thus the coastal areas of West Africa tend to be wealthy, the interior savanna areas are poor; and the latter export their labour to the former. (These contrasts account, in part, for the striking differences in national *per-capita* incomes; thus Ghana (£99), has a relatively small savanna population compared with that of Nigeria – £29.) The wealthy areas have higher educational levels and tend to supply literate clerks and teachers to the poorer and backward areas. Inevitably people of the more backward areas begin to feel that they are being exploited by those of the richer areas and because poverty is identified with territory rather than with social class the contest is seen as lying between ethnic groups. Thus in Ghana one reason for the opposition to Nkrumah which developed in the Ashanti cocoa-growing areas was that the wealth from cocoa was being used to develop the capital, Accra, rather than Ashanti itself, and that in Accra the Ashanti people were sharing only marginally in the varied benefits of national independence.

A further and probably more important aspect of economic development is the manner in which income is distributed within the poorer nations. No society known to us is so completely egalitarian that every man receives a similar income. In the western industrialized societies we find that the bottom 50 per cent of the population earns between 20 and 30 per cent of the total income and that the top 10 per cent receives about 30 per cent. In the poorer nations the distribution would seem to be far more uneven than this. (Figures for income, calculated usually from tax returns, are, of course, notoriously unreliable, especially in the poorer nations, yet even allowing for a substantial margin of error the inequality of income distribution does contrast strikingly with that of industrial societies.) In Peru the bottom two thirds of the population earns only 14 per cent of the total income of the country; this category is composed of persons earning less than £125 a year. The top 2 per cent of the population receives over 40 per cent. In Ceylon the disparity is somewhat less striking; the bottom 60 per cent of the population receive 25 per cent of the income; the top 10 per cent receive 40 per cent. It is probably true that, in these poorer countries, the richest 10 per cent or 2 per cent of the population receive a higher proportion of the natural income than the same categories in industrial nations. The unevenness of distribution is, furthermore, probably greater in Latin American countries where substantial incomes are gained in landowning and business; correspondingly it is least in Africa where such incomes tend, today, to be negligible in comparison and the rich are, to a far greater degree, the senior civil servants, professionals and politicians.

The inequality of income can be expressed, too, in the range of incomes from the very poor to the very rich. This is great in most societies but in the poorer nations the differences seem very wide. Thus in Peru half the population earns less than £60 a year while the richest 2 per cent receive an average income of £4,000 a year. Characteristic of these societies is the very large proportion of the population, both rural and urban, at the lowest income levels. It seems likely, too, that the richest men display their wealth with greater ostentation than their counterparts in industrial societies; they have large estates and city mansions, and often collect a following of clients. Again the relative paucity of people in the middle-income brackets makes the contrast between rich and poor seem more striking.

Ultimately more important than the statistical range of incomes in any society is the attitude of its members to the inequality. How legitimate are the incomes of the rich in the eyes of the poor? Are incomes from landowning, business or the professions seen as the result of exploitation of the poor or as the reward for merit and ability? Inasmuch as those now receiving high incomes have only recently reached this social status, is their route of upward mobility accepted as legitimate? Should, for instance, the rewards of political office be commensurate with those of academic achievement? These are all questions which we must examine again later in discussing the relationship between the élites of the poorer nations and the masses.

In some respects the poorer nations of today resemble the western nations at the period when rapid industrial development was about to begin. The proportion of the population engaged in agriculture is high; the patterns of income distribution are perhaps similar. But as the foregoing paragraphs have shown the economic development of the poorer nations, by the large companies of the industrial nations, is very different from the growth of small private businesses in Britain and western Europe in the seventeenth and eighteenth centuries. Furthermore, and this is our next theme, the poorer nations today expect, and are expected, to emulate the style of government and level of social services which have developed in the past two centuries in the industrial nations.

DEMOCRACY AND WELFARE

Throughout Latin America, Asia and Africa a substantial measure of democracy (that is, popular participation in political matters) normally occurred at the local level of the district and village; but at a higher level it was absent. In much of tribal Africa the larger political units did not exist; in Latin America and Asia power rested with a small ruling aristocracy. Today in these countries universal adult suffrage is the general practice. In the colonial territories of Africa and Asia elected government was seen as a prerequisite of independence both by the departing colonial administrators and by the nationalist intellectuals who wished to demonstrate that they had a popular following. In the Latin American countries the right to vote was generally restricted, in the nineteenth century, by sex, and educational and property qualifications. By 1936 most of the latter qualifications were removed in Colombia and in 1954 women were granted the vote. But there was still apathy in registering and in 1962 a million Colombians, most of them women, still did not have the vote.

The impact of these recent innovations has been that the masses, however ignorant or misconceived they may be about the political process, at least feel that they have a stake in it, if only to express a vote for or against the ruling political party at infrequent elections. The rivalry between political groups is no longer restricted to competition between cliques within a ruling aristocracy or within the intellectual élite of a colonial territory; politicians must woo their electorates, promising them rewards for their support and making at least some pretence of recognizing their demands. The political parties thus created a new avenue by which men from the lower social strata may reach positions of power. Furthermore, at the local level a new role has emerged – that of broker: the man who does not immediately aspire to high office but seeks rewards in a variety of forms in return for his ability to deliver the votes of his clients and followers. These brokers are usually men of substance in their own communities and their demands are an increasingly important constraint upon the policies of the nationalist leaders.

Secondly, the sphere of competence of the present governments of the poorer nations is much greater than that of their counterparts in pre-industrial Europe. We have already seen that the governments in the poorer nations do not control the large companies which dominate their economy, except by indirect means such as cajolery and ultimately by nationalization. But they do control substantial sections of the economy. The African states are extreme in this case for the development of public services – railways, and electricity undertakings – was carried out by the colonial governments and control has now passed to the indigenous political leaders. In some states, such as Ghana, the government took the initiative in developing new industries. But everywhere it is accepted that economic development is ultimately the responsibility of the government rather than the private businessman. A corollary to the situation is that the government is the major employer of labour. Thus in most African states (save those with a dominant mining industry) a half or more of the wage-earners are employed in the public sector; and a far higher proportion of the well-educated are so employed. In such a situation the grievances of the wage-earners are directed towards the government and its leaders; they become expressed in a political form; the politicians are not able to assume the role of arbitrators between wage-earners and employers. This has led to attempts to control the trade unions, incorporating them perhaps into the dominant political party.

Thirdly, leaders of the poorer nations today have a much greater coercive power than their counterparts two centuries ago. The English magistrate in a small provincial town, faced with rioting peasants or townsmen, might have waited for several days for the arrival of the militia; for his own safety he had to parley and compromise. How different must a peasant rebellion be today when a government can, within hours, fly in American-trained and equipped troops. The governments of the nineteenth-century Latin American nations and the pre-colonial Indian states had substantial armies, though equipped with relatively simple weapons. In recent years the armies of Latin America have been completely modernized through the assistance of several of the western industrial nations. (Nowadays, U.S. aid is most marked but Bolivia, for instance, in the 1930s, relied on German help.) In the colonial countries indigenous officers were

55

trained in the military academies of the metropolitan country, creating a relationship which has been sustained in the post-colonial period. Governments can thus control the masses of their country. But the power of the military leaders is equally a threat to the party political leaders. Recent coups have shown how easy it is, given a substantial degree of unanimity within the officer corps, for a small number of soldiers to seize the important public buildings in the capital and replace one set of leaders by another. We see here a competition for power between different groups within the national élite. Tension can, of course, exist even within the army, for instance between the junior officers, with a superior degree of professional training, and their superiors. Lastly, the army, like the modern political party, may constitute a new route to positions of power within the society emphasizing different criteria for recruitment from either those of leadership within the political party or academic achievement in bureaucratic posts and the professions.

In the modern sector of the economy, education is a basic qualification. The level of schooling is one of the major factors affecting appointment and promotion in the bureaucratic structure; a minimal education is demanded from the most lowly wage labourer. Thus, with the realization of this situation and the awareness that mobility into the modern sector is possible, the masses have begun to demand a rapid expansion of primary education. Furthermore, among the political leaders there is one school of thought which argues that economic development is only possible when the mass of the population is literate. Politicians, wooing the electorates for support, must promise either increased social services or the termination of abuses – through land reforms, for instance. In areas such as ex-colonial and tribal Africa the emphasis must be on the former for here there is little else that the politician can promise. In all the poorer nations schools existed to train the small élite, either perpetuating the ruling aristocracy or providing the colonial power with an administrative cadre. In recent decades the expansion of education has been phenomenal. Thus in the southern regions of Nigeria universal primary education was instituted in the 1950s. In India, in the same period, most boys received some primary education – though only half as many girls. In Colombia, for instance, by 1958 most children started primary schooling; the number in primary schools had more than doubled in the previous two decades. But against this picture of almost universal entry to the lowest class of the primary school must be set the high drop-out rate, it being variously reported that in Colombia only 13 per cent, in India only a third and in Western Nigeria, for instance, less than half of the pupils complete the five or six years of schooling. This drop-out rate may be explained by the costs of schooling – even where tuition is free, books and uniforms must perhaps be bought – and the disillusion of parents with the employment prospects of the not-too-bright child.

This emphasis on the provision of primary schooling poses problems for the governments of the poorer nations. Its cost is very high, especially because such a high proportion of the population is juvenile – nearly half under fifteen years being usual. Furthermore, it stimulates emigration to the towns for it is felt that the rural areas offer no new opportunities for literates with their horizons widened, their traditional values often assailed. Again, the rapid expansion of education leads to a continual rise in the levels required for specific occupations and the migrant is frustrated with his inability to attain the status and salary initially expected by him and successfully achieved, in fact, by kinsmen but a few years older than himself. It is argued that primary schooling should educate the youth for employment in the rural areas instead of stressing, as heretofore, those academic subjects which formed the foundation for an élitist education in secondary schools and universities. But it is difficult for men trained in one system to design the other. Furthermore, provision of a dual system of primary education is not welcomed by the masses who are unwilling to see the future of their children determined, at the age of five years, probably by the economic status of their parents.

Secondary and university education has expanded in a similar manner, in response to popular demand with the rising output of the primary schools and to estimates of manpower requirements in the developing nations. The latter however are often calculated with greater emphasis upon the supposed prerequisites for development than upon the investment available for industrial and agricultural expansion. An over-production of secondary-school-leavers can then result in a further educational expansion at a higher level to reduce, for a time, the level of unemployment. At present the poorer nations tend to be producing school- and, in India especially, university-leavers at a greater rate than they can be absorbed in employment.

These expanding systems of education are generally state-controlled and are substantially subsidized; primary education is free in many states and in higher education nominal fees and scholarships reduce the costs to the parents. But these egalitarian factors are countered by others. The secondary-school fees, often for boarding as well as tuition, still place these beyond the reach of children from half or more of the homes in the country. As the number of schools increases so often does the proportion of free places decrease. Thus while many youths from poor homes have, in past years, been enabled to receive both secondary and university education, the children from the wealthier homes now have far higher chances of entering these schools and colleges, because their parents can afford the fees and because with their home background and better primary schooling they more frequently pass the entrance examinations. Educated parents tend to ensure that most or all of their own children are educated and are able to achieve the same or higher social status as themselves. In Africa we find that, after a period when most of the children in secondary school came from traditionally oriented rural homes, the educated élite is increasingly able to dominate these schools and the universities. The Brahmins in India and the aristocracy in Latin America have continued to dominate the seats of learning.

With education the masses of the poorer nations have also demanded improved health facilities – new maternity centres and dispensaries, more urban hospitals. The consequence: a rapidly increasing population largely as a result of the decline in infant mortality. With half of the population under fifteen years of age the costs of social services for the young are high. A relatively small proportion of the population is of working age (though these countries have a much smaller proportion of the elderly retired than the industrial nations). An overall rise in national productivity is balanced by the growth in population so that the gain per head, whether expressed as a bald statistic or in terms of an experienced increase in standards of living, is very small.

Thus a gain in gross domestic product of 4 per cent – no mean achievement in the poorer nations – is counter-balanced by a population increase of 2.5 per cent; net gain: 1.5 per cent. Furthermore, this population increase is shared by all strata of society. Detailed demographic studies are few; in Ghana for instance a slight but perceptible decline in the birth-rate has been detected among the better educated; but the completed family of the fertile woman is still of five or six children. Thus, with the educational system favouring the children of the affluent, the present upper strata can fill, a generation hence, two or three times the number of high status positions at present available. Will the economic development of these countries provide an even greater number of positions?

For many writers the widespread acceptance of birth-control techniques is a prerequisite for economic development. While this might reduce the rate of population increase and might make increased saving possible, it would not alter the structure of society in the poorer nations nor alter their relationship with the industrialized West. Furthermore, one needs to be sure that those who practise the birth-control techniques do so to reduce the total number of offspring – and not merely, as some evidence indicates, to space them more conveniently or to permit sexual intercourse where it was previously avoided.

The nations of the tropics have been characterized in dualistic terms. The culture of the West contrasts strikingly with that of the many indigenous peoples. The market-oriented economy of the modern sector contrasts with the technologically simple agriculture of the rural sector. Men who work in the modern sector and appear substantially to accept western values contrast with the traditionally oriented farmer and craftsman. The skyscrapers of the towns contrast with the mud and thatch huts of the countryside. The gap between the two is seen as increasing rather than narrowing. But it is seen in cultural terms and not in terms of social stratification with wealth and power as the main variables. Thus the interdependence between the two is under-stressed and even denied. The one cannot exist, however, without the other. And the individual members of these societies are not only aware of both aspects but are continually trying to exploit them. The university graduate civil servant, for instance, aspires to a style of living similar to that of men in the industrial nations who have a similar education; but he can still be proud of his own cultural heritage and may, as in Africa, continue to retain strong ties with the village of his birth. The villager may be poor and backward, but radio and newspaper political campaigns all increase his awareness of the wider world. Growing numbers migrate temporarily to the towns returning to the villages with new ideas and new goods. Wars, usually inadvertently, have enabled the lower strata to demand full rights of citizenship. Thus Africans who fought in the Middle East and Asian campaigns of the Second World War were subsequently active in the independence movement. In Bolivia the awakening of Indian consciousness is attributed to the Chaco war with Paraguay in 1932 in which they played a prominent role.

The picture of the limited but promising economic development of the 1950s has, in the 1960s, turned to one of gloom and stagnation. The experience of individual countries and of regions within countries is, of course, varied; there is a boom in one commodity, a slump in another. But the overall pattern is one in which the western industrial nations seem to be drawing even further ahead of the poorer nations. In the first seven years of the 1960s Latin America's *per-capita* income rose by only 1·7 per cent; its share of world trade fell from 8·5 to 5·7 per cent; its share of imports into the U.S.A. fell from 31 per cent to 16 per cent. As the industrial nations become even more technologically advanced, so are their links with each other strengthened at the expense of the raw material producing countries. Thus while Latin America's share of U.S. overseas investment fell from 26 per cent in 1960 to 18 per cent in 1967, that of Europe rose from 21 per cent to 31 per cent. Notwithstanding overseas investment in manufacturing industry in the poorer nations, the attractions provided by the richer countries are stronger. The 1960s saw, too, a decline in the amount of aid which passed from the industrial to the poorer nations. Furthermore, the terms on which it was given were increasingly adverse; most U.S. aid to Latin America had to be spent on purchases from the U.S.A. Little wonder that the poorer nations saw aid as being distributed in the interests of the donors rather than the recipients. Declining aid and economic stagnation are held responsible for the sudden nationalization in 1969 of U.S.-owned extractive industries in Latin America – oil and sugar in Peru, copper in Chile – and of the copper-mines of Zambia. When partnership with the industrial nations seemingly yields decreasing rewards, the outright seizure of their assets to control the distribution of profits seems the most attractive course. Yet one must not kill the goose that lays the golden eggs. To ruin an industry which dominates the national economy would mean increased unemployment and poverty.

What matters to men and women in any society is not so much the statistically demonstrated rise in *per-capita* incomes but the increased standard of living which they themselves experience compared both with their own previous standard and with the changing standards enjoyed by others around them. To generalize again across nations is clearly impossible here; in each country a distinct pattern will emerge, but too few studies have been made to give even a comparative picture. However, Rosen's study of changes in the economic position of different categories of persons in post-Independence India provides an excellent example.[1] In the urban sector he estimates that two categories have gained most – those with high incomes in the private sector and the skilled and organized factory-worker; these have benefited from the expansion of industrial growth. Conversely the high income government employees have lost both absolutely and in relation to other categories – but this loss is countered by the fact that individuals will have received promotion and will not therefore have suffered a real decline in incomes. The real incomes of the lower white-collar workers and the unskilled working class have probably remained stationary. The former see themselves more distantly separated from the higher income categories whom they aspire to emulate; they are frustrated by the failure of their education to bring them the expected rewards; they feel threatened by the relative affluence of the skilled worker. This category can therefore harbour extreme discontent which may lead its members to demand revolutionary political change or to identify class with caste interests and to support communal partners and movements. The stagnant incomes of the unskilled workers, together with the rapidly rising urban unemployment – threefold in a decade – has tended to reduce the immigration into the urban areas. In the rural areas the redistribution of land has not only helped to stabilize the population but has also restructured the pattern of rural incomes. It is the middle-income peasants who have gained most, however. The landowners, who themselves farmed little or none of the land, lost land in the process of redistribution, though many were able to evade expropriation by placing their holdings in the nominal ownership of relatives. The incomes of landless agricultural labourers, still at 20 per cent a large proportion of the rural population, remained stationary. The bigger farmers were able to take advantage of new techniques to increase their output; the smaller farmers acquired land or were relieved of the burdens of rents and dues.

In the current decades we are said to be witnesses of the 'revolution of rising expectations'. What is significant is not that millions of men and women in poor tropical countries are discovering that a better life, as enjoyed by their own compatriots in the affluent urban suburbs and by the people of industrial countries, might also be enjoyed by themselves. It is that their aspirations are, to an increasing degree, being frustrated as their own living styles remain unchanged and as the chances that they or their children will attain a higher standard of living grow more remote.

4 A Process of Modernization?

With each year the technological gap widens between the space rockets of the industrial nations and the simple tools of the farmer in tropical lands. Yet the high standards of living which western technology sustains are eagerly sought by those in the poorer nations, who, to an ever-increasing degree, both recognize the differences between the affluence of some and the poverty of others, and believe that these differences can and ought to be eradicated. The wealthy and educated élite of the poorer nations have already achieved a style of life which, in its material respects, resembles that of men in similar occupations in the industrial nations. As often as not, however, they are critical of the values which are extolled in the West, categorizing these as materialistic; the vehemence with which they assert the traditional values of their own particular societies may none the less be due to the pressure on these as they are found to be increasingly incompatible with their new style of life. For the poorer people the mere acquisition of a radio, a bicycle or a sewing-machine is much less of a threat to their existing values and patterns of social relationships. The goals of all the people of the poorer nations are thus expressed in terms of technology and of living standards; for the majority the goal is not to replicate western patterns of behaviour. This distinction must be clearly recognized. The African university lecturer lives in a campus house furnished almost identically with that of his European colleague; he may nevertheless maintain a very different pattern of relationships with his wife, children and close relatives.

The cultural differences between the poorer nations and the variety in the historical circumstances through which they have been brought into the orbit of the western nations would seem to invalidate the development of a theory which outlined a uniform process of change. Yet the common technological goal of these nations and the growing pervasiveness of a common style of life among the élite of the world have encouraged the formulation of such theories.

Though the terminology of these theories may differ we must clearly distinguish between economic growth and development, and between change in economic and social spheres. Growth implies a rising national income without any concomitant change in the economic structure; thus the production of a given export commodity may rise – more local industries may be established without substantially affecting the dominance of foreign capital, the dependence upon the industrial nations, the economic inbalance between primary, secondary and tertiary sectors. Development occurs when these and other similar factors are altered. Growth and development are clearly related; economic growth may provide the opportunities for development; development may be a prerequisite for continued growth. But the relationship is, over a short period, not inevitable. Leonard Barnes has compared the economies of Guinea and the Ivory Coast, near neighbours in West Africa.[1] The latter has retained close ties with France and thus has facilitated private capital investment; the economy has grown but not developed. In Guinea the people answered '*non*' to the referendum on continued association with France; the French withdrew precipitately and radical changes were made in the country's economic and political structure; but bereft of capital investment economic production has not grown. The sociological contribution to these discussions of economic growth and development lies for many theorists in the assertion that changes in the economy are paralleled and even dependent upon changes in the entire structure of society. The process of such change is termed modernization.

The critique of modernization theories which follows draws heavily upon the seminal essay of André Gundar Frank;[2] the alternative approach which I propose derives more from recent advances in social anthropology in which emphasis is placed on the role of the individual in altering the structure of institutions, at the expense of the values which maintain it.

Daniel Lerner writes,

Modernization is in my lexicon the social process of which development is the economic component. If economic development produces 'rising output per head', then modernization produces the society and environment in which rising productivity is effectively incorporated.... I would consider as modernized a society that is capable of 'self-sustaining growth' over the long run.[3]

He continues,

There is a simple process of modernization which operates in all developing societies, regardless of their colour, creed or climate and regardless of their history, geography or culture. This is the process of economic development; and since development cannot be sustained without modernization, I consider it appropriate to stress this common mechanism underlying the various forces of modernization.[4]

Lerner accepts that cultural and historical differences may 'modify the development process, by varying its mode and adjusting its tempo. But they cannot change the basic mechanism underlying the peculiarities of mode and tempo.'[5] He confesses that he feels that modernization is neither desirable nor feasible for all countries at the present time; but in so far as their leaders have accepted this as their goal they must acknowledge the demands of the process.

Other writers are less dogmatic. Yet common to their approaches is the notion of evolution. Societies are not merely changing but are evolving. This implies either a change towards a higher form already determined or a continuing adaptation to the environment. The two aspects may be related, yet it is the former which is usually stressed. Thus for Parsons evolution is denoted by the process of 'structural differentiation' as institutions become more complex and more highly specialized. It is not clear in his writings how this change is effected – he is describing a direction of change rather than a process.[6]

The evolutionary component in sociological theories of modernization is paralleled by popular attitudes in western nations. We so often speak of the poorer nations trying to 'catch up' western nations; and we argue that as it took us several centuries to reach our present position from that point at which the poorer nations seem now to be, so will it take them as long – or at best, a little less. In these statements we imply a common goal and a simple route to achieve it.

A further aspect of evolutionary thinking is the inevitability implied in the process. Modernization is bound to occur in the poorer nations though the pace of change may be slow and the tensions great. The undoubted changes which have taken place since the beginning of this century clearly support such attitudes. Yet the retarded growth rates, and even apparent stagnation in the past decade, should at least challenge our self-assurance.

The evolutionary process is presented sometimes in terms of the transition from tradition to modernity, sometimes in terms of stages of development. Let us look at the premises underlying each of these approaches.

The dichotomy between traditional and modern societies is often expressed in terms of Parsons' pattern variables. Thus in traditional societies, status is ascribed by age or birth, while in modern societies it is achieved. In traditional societies social relationships are diffuse, whereas in modern societies they are specific – our relationships with other individuals are in terms of a single interest or sphere of activity and not, as in traditional society of multiple interests. Values in traditional society are particularistic, in modern societies universal. It is held that in both traditional and modern society these and other such attributes are interdependent. Furthermore each attitude may be scaled – the relative degrees of ascriptiveness and achievement may be measured. A society which is modernizing will therefore exhibit to an increasing degree the attributes of the modern society at the expense of those of traditional society. Policymakers who implicitly accept this mode of analysis will therefore support any institution in a developing nation which is based upon the attributes of modernity and will view as retrogressive any which upholds traditional attributes.

Parsons' pattern variables were presented as tools for analysis and the traditional and modern societies so identified were ideal types. Yet it has been only too easy to identify the poorer nations of the world as traditional, the western industrial nations as modern societies. The nations are then scaled on a single dimension. There are, however, a number of fallacies in this approach. Firstly the categorization of the poorer nations as traditional societies imposes a uniformity which does not exist. We have seen for instance in an earlier chapter that achieved status is significant in many tribal African societies such as that of the Ibo people; we can, too, find many instances of ascribed status in our own society. The distribution of these attributes among the societies of the world follows a very complex and irregular pattern. Secondly the placing of societies on a scale of tradition – modernity implies a uniformity of norms and values within these societies; yet differences, as between the wealthier and poorer sections of the population, may easily be seen. The western educated élite in the poorer nations may uphold many more of the values of modernity than the masses; traditional attitudes may be pronounced among the ruling groups in a western nation. If a process of change from tradition to modernity is to have any validity it must be shown that those groups which are assigned the attributes of modernity are in fact those which contribute most to the economic development of their society. It can be argued, however, that in the poorer nations at least, these groups are an impediment to change. A partial explanation of this apparent paradox may lie in the incongruence between the proclaimed values of a society and actual patterns of behaviour. Thus the emphasis of achievement in western industrial society is countered by the ascriptive tendencies of the upper classes, demonstrated in Anthony Sampson's *Anatomy of Britain*.[7]

Lerner's theory of modernization cited above owes much to the stages of economic development proposed by Rostow:[8] the lengthy period of establishing preconditions, the short period of 'take off' and the subsequent era of sustained economic progress when growth becomes virtually automatic. The sociologist enumerates his own conditions necessary for the transition from one stage to the next. What these conditions are, both in the economic and social spheres, is open to much debate. One cannot deny that for every change there will be both necessary and sufficient factors. But one cannot assert *a priori* that these will be of universal application. In much evolutionary writing it is suggested that the patterns of economic development now traced in western Europe from the sixteenth to nineteenth centuries will be replicated in the poorer nations. There seem to be three important fallacies in this argument. Firstly, the impact of the western industrial nations has destroyed many features of the traditional economy of the poorer nations – by destroying

67

indigenous crafts and trading for instance; the poorer nations now have living standards not unlike those of medieval Europe, but their present social and economic structure is very different. Secondly, the poorer nations are already sharing in many of the developments of the industrial nations – in their technology, their forms of government and social services. Thirdly, the development of western Europe rested upon its early exploitation of the tropical world – this process cannot be replicated by the poorer nations (except possibly in so far as the capitals of industrializing nations are seen as exploiting their rural hinterlands).

A number of features seem generally characteristic of these evolutionary theories. They rightly emphasize structural change – for this is the type of change which really interests us. As a result they emphasize, too, the interdependence of institutions in a society, postulating that a change in one will produce adaptive changes in the others. This, too, one must accept. But this approach leads one to an ahistorical bias. A greater concern is shown for the internal structure of the traditional society, at an early stage of development, than for its relationship with the external environment. Change is seen as deriving from processes within the structure rather than as a response to environment and demands. The study of the development of traditional into modern society takes precedence over an examination of the conflict between the two. In setting out the prerequisites of development and modernization attention is focused upon the direction and factors of change rather than on the social processes involved. Inasmuch as experts can claim to know the correct path to the generally accepted goals – higher living standards – so can each minor change be evaluated as progressive or retrogressive. There is a right path and a wrong path to be followed by the poorer nations. As Lerner says, '. . . the modernization of most of the world is going badly – is costing too much for too little benefit – owing largely to the lack of comparative analysis on which rational control of the modernization processes could be based.'[9] He refers to 'the flooding of great urban centres by people who have no work there'.[10]

Implicit in the evolutionary approach is the belief in the increasing transferability of social institutions; as countries adopted the technology of the western nations so they adapt their own social structures to resemble those of the West. This widely held viewpoint is far more deterministic than anything postulated by Marx! The institutions allegedly most susceptible to change in this way are, not unnaturally, those associated with industrial organizations. And as the industries in the poorer nations have been largely established by companies based in the western nations some striking similarities in structure can be expected. But industrial organization in Japan is markedly different; workers for instance tend to be paid according to ascribed characteristics – age and length of service, rather than achieved – their levels of skill. Japanese industry seems to flout some of America's most cherished values, and yet remain highly efficient and technologically progressive. The description given in a later chapter of relationships in an Indian factory reinforces the point that traditional forms of relationships are not necessarily an impediment to efficiency.

Evolutionary patterns outlined by western sociologists are, frankly, highly ethnocentric. It seems to be confidently assumed that the rest of the world will not only become like the United States but that it wishes to do so. Here again we must reiterate our distinction between technology and material styles of living on the one hand and patterns of social behaviour on the other. With modern communications, an international style of élite living *is* being diffused throughout the world. But behavioural patterns are by no means concomitant with this. This is not to deny, however, that the men and women of the poorer nations, inasmuch as they do become part of the western society playing an active role in its economic system, do share in its values. Yet, as the Japanese example demonstrates, this is not necessary in order to enjoy the benefits of advanced technology. One might describe these evolutionary theories as culturally imperialistic.

Evolutionary theories, as I have already said, tend to describe the direction rather than the process of change. Of the many themes which ascribe modernization to a single factor, those which describe the role of the entrepreneur are among the most popular and influential. Here, too, we find a streak of ethnocentricism; for at its most extreme it is argued that nineteenth-century economic development in Britain was due to the Victorian middle classes and to the businessmen in particular. One writer states that the Parsonian attributes of modernity – universality, achievement orientation and functional specificity – are 'little more than liberalism re-cast into technical sounding jargon'.[11] Thus the development of the poorer nations is similarly seen to rest with their middle class of businessmen and professionals. One obvious rejoinder here is that the scope for the small capitalist in these nations is very limited; on the one hand he has to compete with the large expatriate companies; on the other the government itself is taking a more dominant part in controlling and even sponsoring economic development. Again, as we shall see later, the business and professional groups in the poorer nations are not necessarily active in promoting change; they may instead be passively defending their existing privileged positions. Nevertheless the positive role of the middle-class entrepreneur continues to be emphasized and governments are evaluated in terms of the control exercised by this category of persons, and it is they who are often most favoured by aid-giving policies.

Sophisticated variants on this theme have been put forward by David McClelland, psychologist, and Everett Hagen, an economist.[12] McClelland holds that entrepreneurial activity is associated with a personality quality which he terms need-achievement; this is defined as competition with an internalized standard of excellence. It is closely allied with and in fact derives from Weber's concept of the protestant ethic – the motive force of the early capitalist period. Thus the rate of economic growth and development will, according to McClelland, be faster in those societies in which the levels of need-achievement are high; in any society the individual with a high need-achievement is more likely to become an entrepreneur. The people of the poorer nations are said to be low in need-achievement; the task is therefore to raise these levels. Need-achievement is acquired through the pressure put upon the child by his parents, and particularly by his mother, for self-reliance; ideally therefore, a society can be transformed through its educational systems with teachers, in lieu of parents who are still dominated by traditional values, instilling the new attitudes into the young. Such a project would be extremely costly. However, associates of McClelland have established courses in Uganda and India where the quality of need-achievement is instilled into promising businessmen as an aid to their future success. McClelland has been challenged both on the interpretation of his own vast data, and upon his definition of need-achievement which associates it so closely with entrepreneurial effort to the exclusion for instance of professional attainments and which omits other motivating forces, such as need-affiliation – the desire to be esteemed by one's fellows. The need-achievement theory not only isolates the individual from his social structure but also from his environment. It predicts success solely in terms of personality and tends to ignore the existence or absence of opportunities which the individual, given specific resources such as wealth and education, might be able to exploit.

Hagen has taken McClelland's theory and set it in a structural framework. His successful entrepreneurs are a social group, probably from the lower ranks of the élite. This group turns to business activity when it feels that its status has been unduly suppressed; it seeks alternative routes to high social status when the existing ones appear blocked by those in power. In its essence, such a theory has been propounded by many others before Hagen; it is said to account for the activity of minority groups – the Jews in European cities and the emigrant Chinese in southeast Asia. Hagen supports his thesis with many examples. In Colombia a high proportion of the indigenous businesses have been founded by men from one province – Antioquia. This province has few economic advantages though, as a coffee-producing area, the accumulation of capital was facilitated; Antioquians were, however, rated higher in need-achievement than other Colombians. Hagen suggests possible causes: the Basque origin of the people, the early importance of mining which resulted in the creation of non-family enterprises, and most significantly for him, the feeling of social rejection and status deprivation relative to the rest of the country. But other writers have added to this list: land shortage forced settlers to engage in manual work and induced co-operation; the province had the best preserved municipal institutions, so different from the bureaucratic centralism that plagued the rest of the country; 'the resulting freedom and community spirit, the relatively wide property distribution and the preservation of artisan traditions contributed to the forging of a distinct Antioquian regional character'.[13] To recapitulate an earlier example, Ibo achievement orientation and success has been attributed both to personality, deriving from the stratification pattern (and not to being a submerged group) and to land shortage which impels emigration.

The theories of both McClelland and Hagen provide us with useful insights though neither merits the importance claimed by its authors. When opportunities for innovation arise it seems quite feasible that personality differences will distinguish the man who is prepared to undertake the risks involved from the one who opts for security. The socially marginal man is often the innovator, seeking new channels through which to assert himself. Equally a socially accepted and perhaps élite group can innovate in order to maintain its position. The description given in the next chapter of the introduction of irrigated farming in a south Indian village supports this proposition. To conclude, innovation must be explained in terms of *several* variables which will be listed below. Innovation furthermore is not restricted to economic activity. In societies where political power is constricted by a landowning aristocracy the alternative route to wealth and high prestige is often through business; but the emerging African western-educated élite, denied political power by the colonial status of their country, turned not to business – an avenue closed for reasons already given – but to the independent professions and the organization of nationalist political parties. The dominant role predicated for private businessmen in the economic development of the poorer nations seems, thus, to have been grossly misconceived.

Evolutionary theories are, principally concerned with the *direction* of change; we have criticized them on the grounds that traditional societies are far more varied in their structure than these theories admit and that there is a strong ethnocentric bias towards a belief in the convergence of institutions in industrial and hence modernized societies – a bias which is not borne out by studies of societies such as Japan. Theories dealing with the role of achievement-oriented entrepreneurs or of categories of men who turn to entrepreneurial activity are describing simple factors of change; they tend to ignore other factors which would seem, *a priori*, to be important. Nevertheless for both types of theories a predictive value is claimed. In the evolutionary scheme societies progress along a predetermined continuum. Studies purport to show significant statistical correlations between given factors of change and specific outcomes. These theories however are least explicit in describing the *process* of change.

The study of the social process is the most complicated mode of analysis. It involves the examination of an infinite number of variables, the relationship between which we understand most imperfectly and many of which are scarcely susceptible to measurement. The computer now enables us to make the necessary complex calculations – but we are still at the stage of discovering in the most elementary way how we might write a programme and what data to feed into the computer. However it is this task which we must try to master instead of relying on the facile and often intriguing theories based upon inadequate or erroneous premises.

THE ROLE OF THE INDIVIDUAL

Structural change is created through the actions of the individual. In all societies the institutional structure is undergoing at least a slow adaptation; on occasion external factors, not specifically the product of any process internal to the society, provide totally new situations – such of course is the impact of the western industrial nations on the tropical world. The individual continually seizes the opportunities thus presented to him, exploits them in his own interest, and in so doing possibly changes the structure of his society, inasmuch as he redefines some norm of behaviour or creates a new status. In making the individual the focus of our study we depart radically from the institutional focus of most theories of modernization.

The study of the social process seems, in fact, to demand that we move to a different level of analysis. In focusing upon the institutional structure the sociologist has studied a pattern of relationships between statuses. It is the norms of behaviour, underpinned by the values of the society, which here are basic. The individual acts according to the norms expected of him; the motivation for deviance from the norms has tended to be explained in terms of his own personality – and hence to fall within the province of the psychologist. Again the individual is seen as the incumbent of one or a few statuses in a limited number of institutions. Sometimes the role expectations of two statuses are incompatible – for instance the expectations of members of an African village of their chief contrast with those of the colonial administrative officer. The tension created within the individual in such situations has, indeed, often been studied but these studies tend to give the individual a passive role; he substantially accepts the role as defined by the stronger party – the administrative officer – or opts out altogether, perhaps becoming an alcoholic within his compound. We are not usually shown the chief manipulating the new situation to enhance his own power and that of his office.

A theory, a framework of analysis, which focuses upon the institutions of society is naturally bound to study the processes which maintain the structure (even though a process which explains stability must *ipso facto* explain change); the emphasis is placed upon the equilibrating tendencies, the continual adaptation of the institution to external factors. What is most difficult to explain in such terms is the sudden destruction of an institution. Thus sociologists have been able to cope with changes in family structure, since the family, so it seems, is almost always with us. But they have failed to know how and why a revolutionary movement overthrows, for instance, a monarchical and aristocratic form of government, replacing it by something completely new – at least in terms of the political statuses created, for there may nevertheless be a continuity in some of the basic traditional values of the society.

The currently growing interest in the role of the individual in change, stems not so much from the most popular sociological theories of the recent one or two decades but from a statistical development namely games theory, and from the study of decision-making by the management economists. The former has provided the tools for the latter. Inasmuch as we can now see the individual making choices which are governed by his own position in the structure of his society and the opportunities presented by the society, we can retrieve the individual from the realms of psychology as a proper focus for sociological study.

Institution-oriented theories – and most of those dealing with modernization and evolution fall into this category – focus upon the norms and values of the society, not only stressing the inter-dependence of these, but also implying a consensus as to their validity. Theories oriented towards the individual interpret his behaviour in terms of his interests and goals and those of one individual inevitably conflict with those of others; for even when two or more men with common interests co-operate, it is usually against a third with different interests. How do we define a man's interests? Basically I would see these in terms of power and wealth – a man seeks to increase his own share of these scarce resources either absolutely and/or relative to that of others. This viewpoint is often attacked as materialistic by those who would see men's actions determined almost exclusively by their intern-alized value of their society. At worst the two explanations are but equally biased. And it can be shown, I think, that values are often stressed as a motivating force by those whose aspirations to higher status in terms of wealth have been frustrated; this is the 'I'm poor but honest' syndrome. The goals of any individual are conditioned by the society in which he lives. The opportunities which he perceives are those presented by the structure of the society; the values which he holds will be, to some extent at least, those common to members of the society. Most men aspire to goals already recognized by their society; for instance they seek an office in an established hierarchy and expect to fulfil the expected role, but a few will pursue their interests through the redefinition of established roles or the creation of new statuses. It is in the acceptance, or institutionalization, of these redefined roles and new statuses that structural change occurs.

Not only are the goals of the individual conditioned by the society of which he is a member but so are the methods by which he achieves these. Individual interaction is seen as a game in which the basic elements in decision-making are the resources of the individual: in terms of wealth, education, skill, personality, etc., and his expectations of the reactions of others, in terms of the sanctions of reward and punishment which they can or will wield over him. The individual probably plays not alone but in co-operation with others with like interests and goals and in coalition with those whose own goals may differ but can be achieved, apparently, through common action. In this context

75

values are not a determinant of behaviour but a weapon used by contestants; thus they may justify their actions in terms of values which are accepted by the opponent, so that he is placed in a position of accepting the legitimacy of actions which are counter to his own self-interest.

The social process, defined in these terms as a game, or series of games, between individuals does not predict any specific direction of change, nor indeed does it predict that change will occur. The outcome of any single game depends upon a large number of specific factors or variables, the values for which are a matter for empirical inquiry. These determine the outcome of the game and might as well result in the maintenance of the *status quo* as in a structural change of either a slight or a radical character.

The approach which I have indicated so cursorily in the foregoing paragraph is, of course, appropriate to the study of social stratification, which I have arbitrarily selected as the theme of this book. For in each case the basic premiss is the unequal distribution of power, wealth and prestige in society and the attempts made by individuals and groups to increase their absolute and relative shares. In the pages which follow I shall show how individuals and groups have tried to exploit new situations, basically resulting from the western impact, to their own advantage and often in opposition to others whose status is menaced by these developments. Succeeding chapters will demonstrate situations involving the rural peasantry, the urban migrant and the new national élites, culminating in the attempts made by the existing élites to preserve their privileged positions while appearing to accede to the demands of the masses.

Such situations could in most cases be termed ones of class conflict. Yet in the poorer nations – and especially those of Africa and Asia, but less so in Latin America – the concept of class is alien to most of the population. Ideologies of national unity and consensus are successfully promoted and conflicts are frequently expressed in ethnic terms. Yet, as I hope to illustrate, these merely disguise conflicts of interest expressed in terms of power and wealth.

To describe the process of social change in terms of class conflict suggests an acceptance of a Marxist analysis. Marx, however, was an evolutionary thinker, typical of his time, and his progression of society through a series of stages with the lower classes in each eventually overthrowing the upper, has an air of inevitability despite Marx's emphasis on the role of the individual in exploiting each new situation. The intensification of the class struggle leading to revolution does not always occur (and has occurred where Marx least expected it). In industrial societies the general rise in living standards and the belief in the existence of an open society (notably of course by the so-called middle class) have militated against the development of a stronger class consciousness in spite of the fact that the distribution of wealth remains as unequal as it was half a century ago. Again South Africa provides an example of a society where strong antagonisms undoubtedly exist, but where the physical power wielded by the dominant group is so great that realists have ceased to expect an imminent revolution by the Bantu. Marx's theory of class struggle is however inseparable from his concept of the contradiction between the means of production – the technological environment, and the mode of production – the social pattern of relationships. Here, too, an inevitability of change is suggested which is difficult and perhaps impossible to substantiate empirically. However, the emphasis placed here on the technological environment does correct the bias of sociological theories which attempt to study change as a process internal to the institutional structure of society. Reformulated, the Marxist thesis might run: the environment facilitates the development of social relationships which, if actualized, would directly threaten the existing institutional order. But the actualization of these relationships will depend on the success with which groups having vested interests in the maintenance of the social order are able to cope with threats to their status by less privileged groups. The measures taken by these various groups *may* result in the actualization of the new social relationships leading to a change in the institutions of the society; but conversely they may be compensatory, leaving the institutions intact – though not removing the source of the contradiction. As thus expressed, change is not inevitable. Attempts which have been made to reintroduce the idea of inevitability have not, in my opinion, been sufficiently convincing. Thus a biologist, thinking in terms of genetics writes of a slow accumulation of quantitative changes leading to a sudden qualitative change.[14] A historian writes of 'over deter-mination' in analysing the inability of the Russian nobility in the beginning of this century to cope with the problems caused by the 'contradictions' between the modern technology being intro-duced and the feudal social relationships.[15] With our present knowledge of the process of social change these concepts have a value in describing past events but are of little use in predicting them. When the revolution succeeds we say that conditions were ripe for it; if it fails, then they were not yet ripe! Increasing knowledge of social processes will help us to predict the outcome of social conflicts; but inasmuch as this knowledge is also avail-able to the participants, it will condition their own response to each situation.

In conclusion the pattern of social changes taking place in the poorer nations today may have a certain uniformity at the higher levels of abstraction; but such pattern seems unlikely to illumin-ate substantially our understanding of everyday events nor will it be of much use in social engineering. Theories of modernization too, based as they are upon evolutionary nations or single factors, would seem to be unprofitable. The social process rests upon a highly complex set of variables from which, in our present state of knowledge, we can neither predict future events with any degree of accuracy nor determine any general direction of change. Our task, therefore, is to increase our knowledge through empirical study.

5   The Rural Scene

The impact of western technology upon the poorer nations is, of course, most apparent in their rapidly growing capitals and industrial centres, in their affluent élites and, too, in the poverty-stricken inhabitants of the shanty-towns. But, as we have indicated already, the rural areas are not unaffected by the ongoing changes. Their economy is interdependent with that of the towns; a strong migratory flow links the populations of city and village; newspapers and the radio are bringing new ideas to the remotest settlements. Traditional modes of behaviour are giving way, albeit often slowly. Let us start therefore with a description of changes taking place in the rural areas; for, in looking at a small community, it is possible to see more clearly the impact of technological innovations and the like. Within the village one can study the exploitation of new resources by individuals, and the tensions produced by the ensuing structural changes in the society – themes which we will take up again in later chapters, but on a larger scale, when we discuss the roles of new urban groups.

I shall now examine the changes in the rural scene from three angles. Firstly, I shall demonstrate, with an example drawn from a study of two near-by villages, the social changes consequent upon the introduction of new techniques. Secondly, I shall move from the study of innovation in the small community to consider on a wider scale, the forms of protest which arise when the expectations of the rural farmers are frustrated. Thirdly, I shall examine the impact of land reform on the existing rural society, taking case material from India and Bolivia.

INNOVATION

I have already argued that we must see social change not in terms of some unidimensional pattern of evolution but as a series

79

of responses to specific situations – the new opportunities provided by the environment. A brilliant study which emphasizes this theme has been made by Scarlet Epstein in her description of two villages in Mysore, South India.[1]

Wangala and Dalena were, to all intents and purposes, structured in a like manner until a few decades ago. Wangala had a population in the mid 1950s of nearly one thousand while Dalena had seven hundred. In neither village was there a dominant Brahmin caste (as in the Tanjore village described in chapter 2) but peasant castes accounted for two thirds of the population in Wangala and four fifths in Dalena. Both villages had some craft castes, the untouchables accounted for 18 per cent of Wangala's population and 10 per cent of that of Dalena. Most of the land was held by the peasants, the untouchables owning only 7 per cent in Wangala and 2 per cent in Dalena. Prior to 1939 about one eighth of Wangala's land was irrigated in traditional fashion from the village tank. The great change came when the Indian government sponsored a large irrigation scheme; 60 per cent of its land was then irrigated and planted with sugar and paddy rice. The growing of sugar was facilitated by the building of a crushing factory in the near-by town and market centre of Mandya and by the encouragement to grow the new crop given to the farmers by purchasing contracts. Dalena, on the other hand, was located on land too high to be irrigated. But, seeing the rising incomes of their neighbours, its people were spurred into exploiting secondary opportunities which derived from sugar growing, providing services for the irrigated villages, and working in the new factories in Mandya; they were helped inasmuch as Dalena lay by a main road and had electricity.

Over the years the prosperity of both Wangala and Dalena grew to a like degree. In fact the cash income of Wangala from its sales of sugar and rice exceeded that of Dalena, whose farming continued substantially to follow the traditional subsistence pattern. The new occupations taken up by Dalena men, from enterprising entrepreneur to urban labourer, resulted in an increased inequality of income in this village. The picture that emerges from Epstein's fascinating description is that Wangala accepted the innovations but that they necessitated little change in the social structure of the village; in adapting to the new environment it had merely become stagnant at a rather more prosperous level. In Dalena, on the other hand, a series of changes had set in motion a process leading to sustained growth; the village seemed progressive. This difference is most noticeable in the physical appearance of the two villages today.

Wangala still looks like the traditional type of village in the area. Though new houses have been built in recent years and some of them are neatly white-washed, or even elaborately decorated with colourful paintings, their style is unchanged. Habitations are still mud huts or rectangular-shaped mud houses with country-tiled roofs; one half is occupied by the family and the other by the farm animals without any partition whatsoever between the two sections. At night most houses are in complete darkness; the only type of lamp used in Wangala is a tiny oil-lamp. .... If farmers go off to their fields at night to check irrigation flows, they wait until the moon comes up, so that they can see their way.[2]

In contrast Dalena has electric light in its main streets; the first buildings one meets on entering the village are a cane-crusher and a rice-mill. A rich trader has an imposing two-storey house and there are a number of equally modern houses in a new quarter of the village. Dalena has a good water supply from newly constructed wells. Again it should be stressed that the two villages are equally wealthy – the average monthly income per household in Dalena being 36 rupees (or about £2·50) and in Wangala 33 rupees. How has this striking disparity come about?

First let us look at Wangala. We must start by asking which individuals or groups were best placed to take advantage of the new opportunities provided directly and indirectly by irrigation? The cultivation of irrigated land demands four times as much capital and more labour than that of dry land. It is hardly surprising therefore that the innovators in Wangala were the already wealthy farmers. 'Irrigation re-emphasised the economic predominance of the richest farmers. The five richest families today were also the richest before irrigation. These five magnate households had been traders as well as farmers: they had been familiar with the working of a money economy and they had cash available for investment and working capital.'[3] These men possessed land, and through their existing relationships with dependent poor peasants and outcastes had an assured supply of labour.

There were, however, constraints on the degree to which they might increase their dominance in the village. The cane-crushing factory advanced money to farmers which helped them to establish their fields of sugar and also fixed an upper limit of two fields of cane which they agreed to buy. The large joint families got round this limitation by putting fields in the names of junior members – but this hastened the eventual break up of these families into small units. Again little land came on to the market but the few sales and the rather more common pledging of land by the poorer families (including that granted specifically by the government to the untouchables) led to a redistribution in favour of the rich peasants. When irrigation started, some wealthy men, not members of the village, purchased land in the hope of considerable profit; but with the labour of the village poor already committed to their local patrons, these strangers were unable to cultivate their land and after several years re-sold it to local buyers at no great gain.

The members of the craft castes in Wangala are, today, landholders though not on a large scale. But they still practise their crafts. Traditionally they provided services for their patrons in return for a fixed reward of grain and hay; this provided an assurance against the risks of poor harvests but acted as a disincentive in an expanding economy. Wangala's blacksmith was an enterprising man and approached the village council asking that he be allowed to sever all his traditional obligations and work on a purely cash basis. But the village farmers protested that they must have a resident blacksmith for they could not mend their own ploughs; they would accede to his request only if he found a substitute to perform the traditional obligations. If he refused, the village would make life uncomfortable for him. The blacksmith was a landowner and looked to his farm as a security against famine years when people had no money for repairs and also as a source of prestige; he was reluctant to quit the village; so he found a cousin who undertook the traditional obligations while he concentrated on making new tools necessitated by sugar and rice cultivation. This change was facilitated by the fact that the blacksmith had no ritual relationship with the village members. The farmers of Wangala did in fact have less need of the economic services of washermen and barbers than heretofore, but the ritual relationships – the washermen wash menstrual cloths, the barbers have important roles at weddings and funerals – ensured the continuance of the traditional status.

The cash income of Wangala has provided opportunities for shops and eating-houses. These have been exploited successfully by Muslims. These men are on the fringe of Wangala society; they do not participate in the village feasts or the village council; they find it difficult to get casual labour for their farms. Peasants refuse to open shops in spite of the high rewards, for they cannot squat on the floor and offer goods to all passers-by, whether they are untouchables or of lower caste; again the peasant must be charitable to his kin and neighbours and would have to sell on credit – a rather risky venture; the Muslim can sell for cash extending credit only to wage-earners.

The exploitation of the new opportunities offered has been seen in relation to the resources of individuals – in terms of capital, land, control of labour – and to the possible sanctions resulting from alternative courses of action. Let us amplify this picture by looking at some of the apparent opportunities which Wangala men have rejected.

Before irrigation many Wangala men sought wage employment, often far from the village. But these men later returned home to farm. Some men do work on the plantation established in Wangala by the sugar factory but they do so on a part-time basis, continuing to work their own land. Only one Wangala resident works outside the village – he is an illiterate Muslim who only recently immigrated and he keeps his former job as a postman in Mandya while his wife runs a shop.

One might surmise that the shortage of labour at peak periods would result in the development and use of labour-saving tools. But this has not occurred. In fact there is a considerable amount of under-employment in Wangala. Most Peasant households have traditional relationships with untouchable households which oblige them to provide the latter with a minimum subsistence whether or not they use their services; to use them less would mean no saving – in fact the destitute client on one's doorstep would merely advertise one's meanness to the village. Farmers in Dalena adapted an improved practice of rice-planting, termed the 'Japanese method'. This was rejected in Wangala in spite of an admission that it does increase yields. Rice was traditionally planted by teams of labourers who were reluctant to see their organization broken with no apparent increase in reward. The farmer who tried to innovate would probably be unable to get a team at the optimal time and would suffer thereby. This conservatism contrasts with the manner in which the same farmers have adopted many new techniques in cane farming; but cane was a new crop with no established procedures and thus innovation was made easier.

Other opportunities, too, have been rejected in Wangala. Only one third of the pupils attend the local school with any regularity; none of these are girls. It would not have been difficult to bring electricity to Wangala, but there was no demand for it. No efforts have been made to improve the local water supply.

In general, Wangala has increased in prosperity, but the innovations responsible for this have been incorporated into village life so that the adaptations necessitated have produced a minimal structural change. The resources needed to irrigate land were those already possessed by the wealthy farmers. A high prestige already attached to farming so that all in the village aspired to landowning. The marginal Muslims increased their marginality by shopkeeping. As men rose in wealth so they attempted to consolidate their new status through sanskritization – the learning and practice of the traditional religious canons and values. Much of the increased cash income was spent on weddings which became increasingly elaborate and were the most striking expression of economic differentiation between Wangala families; a rich farmer would spend ten times as much as the poorest villager. In contrast status differences were less markedly expressed in clothing, watches, bicycles and the like. Epstein reports that in recent years the proportion of intra-village marriages had increased in Wangala – an illustration of the fact that the growing of a cash crop, though undoubtedly drawing the village into the wider economy, does not necessarily extend its relationships in all spheres.

Often one reads that the values associated with the family are those most resistant to change. Paradoxically in Wangala it is in these relationships that some of the most striking changes have taken place. For another expression of affluence of the wealthier peasants was their demand that their wives should no longer work in the fields (and so the demand for the labour of the poorer peasant women and the outcastes increased). Instead the women looked after the production of milk, butter and eggs, the sale of these commodities constituting an independent income. As the husband tried to increase his prestige by freeing his wife from field labour and by buying her jewellery, so she became less overtly subordinate to him. Epstein reported that there were far more marital quarrels in Wangala than in Dalena.

Irrigation has substantially preserved the pattern of social stratification in Wangala though the gap between the middle and poorer families has widened. Such minor alterations in relative status do however give rise to tensions, especially when a newly gained economic status is not congruent with one's ranking in the political and ritual spheres in which hereditary succession to status prevails. Thus the opposing factions in Wangala are crystallized around two ritually important but economically less successful lineages – the 'conservatives' – and two economically dominant lineages – the 'progressives'. (The constituent units of the factions are usually the lineages, and for a wealthy man to achieve prestige he must act through his lineage.) The economically dominant lineages are comparatively recent arrivals in the village and therefore lack important ritual and political offices; continually their members try to find a place for their lineage in the rituals while the 'conservatives' resist, preserving their privileges. The outcome is that the major village ceremonies are duplicated – a phenomenon apparently unknown in the past.

These factions primarily involve the Peasant caste. But relationships between castes have also been affected. The Potters used to believe that they were equal to the Peasants, though the latter denied this claim and refused to eat in Potters' houses. Now that the Potters are mainly farmers their claims are increasingly recognized by the Peasants – the men inter-dine though the women do not. A Peasant has a permanent liaison with a Potter widow in which the village acquiesces.

The economic changes taking place in Wangala have widened the gap between the Peasants and the untouchables and increased the interdependence of the two groups. In this situation the various government measures to improve the status of the untouchables has been to no avail. The untouchables accept the caste system but rebel against their low position in it; they complain of the lack of economic opportunity open to them and argue that irrigation has brought benefits to the wealthy peasants but not to them. Their dependence upon the latter and the economic sanctions that can be wielded against them tend to stifle their protests. But the Wangala untouchables did attempt a symbolic protest during Epstein's residence in the village. Each year the untouchables performed a play for the whole village in which members took the parts of other castes: but caste rules pervade even the stage and the king in the play may not sit on a throne while his audience is squatting on the ground. Led by an untouchable politician from Mandya, the Wangala groups decided to abolish this rule; the politician promised to get support from untouchables in neighbouring villages and from the District Administration. The players had, as a result of their decision, to rely solely on their own resources and could not beg for funds and costumes from caste households. The village *panchayat* decreed a lock-out on untouchable labour; it was the slack season and this was not very effective. Later it organized a poetry reading supported by the adult education authority. The night of the play was wet and the Administration failed to appear; the Wangala untouchables acted before a small audience of outcastes from their own and neighbouring villages. The *panchayat* continued to enforce the lock-out until it became intolerable for both sides when it was commuted to a heavy fine on all untouchable households. The relationship between the castes and the untouchables was firmly re-established.

In this stagnant situation, village government in Wangala experienced little change. Offices on the *panchayat* council were filled by the heads of the major lineages. But the distinction between major and minor lineages was fluid and wealthy men in the latter could gain recognition for their group. That is to say, there were alterations in the ranking of lineages but not in the village structure. Elections were held in a perfunctory way for the new statutory village *panchayat*, on which an untouchable representative would sit; but the new council never functioned and the traditional *panchayat*, though lacking in statutory authority, continued to run the village. And in fact, despite the call on outside help in the matter of the play, Wangala remained antipathetic to state and national governments and their activities.

Dalena provides a striking contrast. Spurred by the absence of obvious local opportunities, the villagers sought them elsewhere. The rich men purchased irrigated land in other villages, thus increasing their wealth, prestige and also their relationships outside the village. Farming techniques on their own dry land remained largely unchanged but this did provide a surplus of labour for working on the irrigated land. However, in Dalena's specific situation it was preferable to hire this on a cash basis and thus the traditional relationships between Peasants and untouchables were ruptured. The establishment of new economic relationships facilitated other innovations; thus Dalena farmers adopted the Japanese method of rice-planting and were more inclined to fertilize their sugar-cane than were the farmers of Wangala. Thus although Wangala took so much pride in the agriculture it was the 'deprived' neighbouring village which adopted the new practices.

Craftsmen in Dalena have tended to become more mobile though they suffer from the competition of rivals in Mandya. Strikingly, Dalena is lacking in shops and eating-places, apparently due to the absence of possible Muslim entrepreneurs; its two shops are in fact run by Peasants but they stock only a limited range of goods. Dalena has become a centre for the sale of bullocks and for the hire of carts to farmers in neighbouring villages who are too poor to invest in their own.

Many Dalena men now work outside their village. Some of these commute daily to offices and factories in Mandya. The organization of contract labour for road and canal building, which Wangala declined when irrigation came, has been exploited by Dalena men. The contractors have hired those men whom they know to be hard workers, irrespective of castes or kin ties.

Thus the opportunities seized by Dalena men have resulted in a much greater occupational differentiation in the village, a wider networking of personal relationships throughout the neighbouring villages and Mandya and a much greater emphasis upon contractual relationships at the expense of the traditional ties of inter-caste dependence. Nevertheless, Dalena still sees itself as a

87

farming community and savings are invested in land as a source of security and prestige. Thus modern wealth is used to acquire traditional status. And in as much as the Dalena man tries to make the best of both worlds he errs in being neither a good farmer nor a good factory-worker.

Dalena men exhibited their wealth in consumption of goods – fine clothes, watches, fridges and sewing-machines. They spent less than their Wangala neighbours on weddings. Epstein reports that the people of Dalena are highly competitive. They would not co-operate, for instance, to buy an irrigation pump which would serve several farms; the wealthy invest in enterprises which they directly control. Through their experiences in Mandya, Dalena villagers learned of the importance of literacy and a few have sent sons to secondary school in the town. Again the comparatively small need for child labour facilitated school attendance. Yet though Dalena is changing in some spheres, the relationship of the farmer to the land has remained unaltered; and so it is here, rather than in Wangala, that the marital relationship has been least affected.

The diversity of economic opportunities has extended the range of wealth in Dalena. At one extreme are the magnates owning mills and irrigated farms; more wealthy and more numerous than those of Wangala. At the other extreme are the poor; more numerous in Dalena than in Wangala. These differences are becoming more hereditary in Dalena; for while a wealthy farmer might find his land subdivided between many heirs, the wealthy trader ensures, through education, that his children will in turn occupy high-ranking positions. Nevertheless, in Dalena, as in Wangala, the overall stratification pattern has not altered significantly. Those who were rich previously have exploited these opportunities and have further increased their wealth; the untouchables take up the more menial and poorly paid jobs.

Tensions arise however due to incongruences in social ranking according to caste or kin criteria and to occupation and wealth. Lineage solidarity is becoming weakened. The modern houses in the new quarter belong to men of several different lineages who are now neighbours; sub-lineage groups are recognized and provide new leadership roles, some of which have been taken by commuters to Mandya. Epstein gives the example of a young factory-worker of a humble family who married the daughter of the village chairman; the prestige accruing from his urban employment was seen as amply compensating for his lowly lineage status. This young man thus used his urban status to enhance his traditional status in his village; paradoxically the girl's father, though a 'conservative', sought a husband who would look after her in the modern urban style. In another example a young man, member of one of the leading lineages in Dalena and a clerk, did not mix with other lineage mates who were mere factory-workers, as they commuted to Mandya; his aloofness outside the town ultimately affected his relationship with it. Occupational ties can cut across caste ties too. A member of the oil-presser caste, and a factory-worker did not normally mix with his fellow-workers in Dalena, they being peasants and regarding themselves as superior. However, when the factory-workers were on strike the oil-presser was always to be found in one or other group discussing the situation. Few such situations occur with the untouchables for they are usually in the lowest paid jobs. One such Dalena man, an orderly, does not mix with other commuters; he is equally cut off from his outcaste fellows for they are envious of his success in having regular employment. The severe competition among untouchables for employment, now that the security of traditional relationships with peasant families has been broken, seems to so weaken their cohesion as a group as to militate against any concerted protest against the stigma attaching to them. The Dalena untouchables have protested neither through political or economic action nor, as in Wangala, symbolically.

Dalena's factional differences are more rigid than those of Wangala where, since all are farmers, many issues affect everyone equally. The 'progressive' faction is led by a lineage containing several of Dalena's wealthiest men, responsible for most of the innovations in the village. The rest of the community are thus envious of their success and critical of the departure from traditional norms that innovation has demanded. The 'conservatives' seek to uphold the traditional values; they include paradoxically most of the commuters to Mandya who seek to use their wealth and position to gain a higher traditional ranking in the village. But whereas the 'progressives' in Wangala sought ritual office in their village, those of Dalena do not and although there are heated arguments about village ceremonies the outcome is usually not duplication but no ceremony at all. Dalena's headman, leader of the 'progressives' and its prime innovator, sought influence and prestige in the wider social and political system in which his economic interests now lie.

Well before the formal elections for the new *panchayat*, Dalena's village council had been reformed to include its most prosperous and influential citizens; this tendency was confirmed in the elections. But the strength of factionalism has tended to reduce the power of the *panchayat* so that it is increasingly restricted to its statutory duties and has ceased to serve as an assembly for discussing and arbitrating all village affairs.

This description of Wangala and Dalena, though but a brief and inadequate summary of the rich detail given by Epstein, has been given at some length in order to emphasize an important point: that social changes occur not because of generalized changes in values but as responses to specific situations, with the outcomes of one situation ultimately affecting others. This is the lesson of Wangala and Dalena. One should not expect that irrigation always leads to stagnation, nor that a diversity of opportunities promotes progress; each case must be examined individually. But we have seen that each new opportunity calls for a certain pattern of resources and that the exploitation of these opportunities may lead to changes in the social stratification in the community. The tensions created as men try to retain their existing privileges or gain those not previously held may, in turn, lead to structural alterations in the society.

PROTEST MOVEMENTS

Wangala and Dalena have both benefited considerably, in terms of living standards, from the irrigation scheme and the resultant new economic opportunities. Yet, as we have seen, the social changes taking place in these two villages would seem to have heightened the tensions between rival factions – now seen as the 'conservatives', anxious to uphold those values which maintain the traditional status which they either hold or aspire to, and the 'progressives' who seek new avenues to power, new symbols of prestige. In Wangala the outcastes rebelled, claiming (and not without reason) that the technological changes in their village had benefited the Peasants exclusively and that they were as poor as before. Let us turn now from the study of the process of innovation and its tensions to a brief examination of peasant protest movements of a larger scale.

Protest movements result from feelings of relative, not absolute, deprivation. Absolute poverty is in fact impossible to define. The living conditions in the slums of western industrial societies would seem luxurious to most of the inhabitants of the shanty-towns of Africa and Latin American cities. People measure their lot not against absolute standards but in relation to those enjoyed by others and to their own expectations. Four situations may thus be defined. Firstly, living standards may in fact have fallen in recent decades and the farmer measures his current poverty against the better conditions of his youth. Population increase, due in a large measure to improved social services, has produced severe land shortage in many areas so that a man can no longer obtain sufficient land to keep him fully employed throughout the year and to maintain his family in the expected style of life. Sometimes the vacant land into which such farmers would have moved has been appropriated by expatriate settlers farming extensively or for commercial plantations. In the second case, living standards have not fallen but contact with the western world has resulted in a sudden rise in expectations which have not been fulfilled. In some cases, these expectations have been stimulated by the presence of colonial government agents and missionaries – especially the latter; the result is illustrated by the cargo cults of Melanesia described below. In the new African states the politicians have been unable to reward their electorate by freeing them from obligations to landlords, for the farmer has kept for his own use almost the entire product of his farm; instead they have promised a 'Life more Abundant', to cite the slogan of the Action Group of Nigeria – a promise which they have not been able to fulfil. Thirdly, people measure their own shares of wealth and power against that enjoyed by others. The conflict between the hard-working peasant and his landlord, living in affluence on his rents, is easily appreciated. More significant perhaps at the present time is, however, the fourth situation, that of unequal benefit from social changes. The introduction of new techniques and opportunities raises the expectations of all, but as the Indian villages have demonstrated some groups have benefited substantially while others find their life unchanged, and perhaps even less secure.

Notwithstanding the magnitude of their grievances, peasants the world over have been notoriously ineffective in redressing them. As Eric Wolf succinctly writes,

Romantics to the contrary, it is not easy for a peasant to engage in sustained rebellion. Peasants are especially handicapped in passing from passive recognition to political participation as a means of setting them right.

First, a peasant's work is more often done alone, on his own land, than in conjunction with his fellows. Moreover, all peasants are to some extent competitors, both for available resources within the community and for services of credit from without. Secondly, the tyranny of work weighs heavily on peasants: their life is geared to an annual routine and to planning for the year to come. Momentary alteration of routine threatens their ability to face up to the routine later. Thirdly, control of land enables them, more often than not, to retreat into subsistence production if adverse conditions alter their market crop. Fourthly, ties of extended kinship are mutual and within the community may cushion the shock of dislocation. Fifthly, peasants' interests – especially among the poor peasants – often cross-cut any class alignments. Rich and poor peasants may be kinsfolk, or a peasant may be at one and the same time owner, renter, sharecropper, labourer for his neighbours and seasonal hand on a near-by plantation. Each different involvement aligns him differently with his fellows and with the outside world. Finally, past exclusion of the peasant from decision-making beyond the bamboo hedge of his village deprives him all too often of the knowledge needed to articulate his interests with the appropriate forms of action.

Hence peasants are often merely passive spectators of political struggles, or else they long for the advent of a millennium, without specifying for themselves and their neighbours the rungs on the staircase to heaven.[4]

Mass millennial cults which are historically important have almost invariably been movements of the underprivileged. They have constituted desperate attempts of people to find a more effective means of controlling and modifying their environment. One may describe them as excursions into fantasy inasmuch as the ends sought and the means employed would seem to us to lack rationality. However, the beliefs which sustain these cults are but an extreme interpretation of those current in the traditional religion, together perhaps with an admixture of revelationary Christianity. Millennial movements can be forward or backward looking. A classic example of the latter is the Ghost Dance that flourished among the North American Indians in the 1880s. The buffalo of the plains had been almost exterminated and the Indians were confined to reservations, obliged to settle as cultivators and in their failure – often due to poor soils or unfavourable weather – to rely on government rations. A prophet announced that their misfortunes were a punishment from their high god for cultivating – it was he who caused the disappearance of the buffalo. If his followers were to enact a dance on several successive nights and, in the meantime, abstain from all activity which might lead to interpersonal quarrels, the ancestors would reappear, bringing back the buffalo and destroying not only the white man but also those Indians who had not participated in the cult.

In contrast, the Melanesian cargo cults looked to the future. The people had seen the style of life enjoyed by white officials and missionaries and though unable to appreciate the source of the affluence, had aspired to share in it. A belief developed – and quickly spread from one community to another – that the goods sought were in fact made by their own ancestors but had been appropriated by the white men. Prophets announced that on the day of the millennium ships carrying cargoes of these goods would arrive and the people would receive their rightful inheritance. To this end the people built cult houses, warehouses for the cargo, wharves and landing-stages. In addition they often destroyed their livestock and stored crops, and threw away their money. In all, a clear threat to the law and order which the colonial government felt its duty to preserve.

In general these cults seem typical of the colonial situation where expectations have been raised by western contact, both in the sense that a higher material style of life is visible and mission teaching raises hopes of future bliss, but where the rate of economic development nowhere reaches these expectations. Colonial government scarcely provides for any articulation of demands by the ruled through formal channels and may even destroy that previously existing in the indigenous system of government. The disparity in status between whites and the local population is marked; one of the frequent aims of the millennial movement is to restore the self-respect of the latter through equality with the former or their eradication.

Cargo cult movements seem now to be on the decline in New Guinea, as alternative avenues to wealth and power become available. In many societies individual achievement is strongly stressed and local entrepreneurs have exploited the opportunities provided by the introduction of new crops – as farmers, traders and transport owners. Many of these men have in addition become political leaders in the new parliamentary forms of government. Cargo cults were least in evidence in those parts of New Guinea where such opportunities have for long existed and they are becoming less significant in earlier strongholds as economic development proceeds. They still do exist, but the greater part of the population now looks on them with disapproval.

In the twentieth century peasant protest movements are becoming increasingly politicized and secular. One reason further is the spread of formal education and the growing understanding of economic opportunities and modern political processes. Another is the need of various élite groups, dependent upon the ballot-box for their exercise of constitutional authority, to win the support of this large amorphous mass. Thus on the one hand we see an increase in effectiveness in peasant-inspired movements; on the other the intellectuals, urban trade unionists, military leaders have variously sought peasant support to augment their attack upon entrenched ruling groups.

Which social group among the peasantry is most likely to support and sustain a peasant rebellion? Eric Wolf argues that it will be the middle peasantry or the peasantry in a peripheral area beyond landlord control.[5] The poor peasant is so dependent upon his landlord (as in the case of the Wangala outcastes) that his tactical power to rebel is negligible. If he is to do so, he must rely on some external power to constrain that which constrains him – a revolutionary army as in China is such an example. The rich peasant on the other hand exercises local power in co-operation with external power holders and it is in his interest to maintain the political structure. The middle peasant, in contrast, has secure access to his land and cultivates it with family labour; he has the minimal tactical freedom to challenge his landlord. Paradoxically, however, it is just these peasants who are usually seen as the main bearers of the cultural tradition – they are the conservative stratum. But it is this stratum which is usually most vulnerable to economic changes such as price irregularities, and increasing land shortage. The middle peasant, too, tends to have one foot in the town where he might have worked for a period and where he sends his children to school, and one foot in the rural area. He is the transmitter of new ideas to the village – not the landless man who relinquished his ties on emigrating to the town. Thus as Wolf argues 'it is the attempt of the middle and free peasants to remain traditional which makes them revolutionary'.[5] The revolutionary potential of this peasant stratum is enhanced by a number of factors. Peasants in frontier areas are free to rebel against centralized authorities; they are abetted if their homeland is mountainous; ethnic differences from a surrounding population increase the cohesion of the rebels. Each of these factors is demonstrated in twentieth-century peasant risings in Mexico, Cuba and China.

'The peasant rebellions of the 20th century are no longer simple responses to local problems, if indeed they ever were. They are but the parochial reactions to major social dislocations, set in motion by overwhelming societal change.'[6] But movements which are peasant led and inspired tend not to be directed towards the overthrow of the existing state and its dominant social structure. 'Peasants in rebellion', says Wolf, 'are natural anarchists.'[7] They seek a free village without landlords and tax-collectors; they do not seek to control the towns.

India seems to have been relatively free of large-scale movements in which the peasants seized the land, and it has been argued that the caste system inhibited rebellion. However, in Hyderabad communists from the neighbouring state of Andhra (where they were established among a landowning caste) started work in the early 1940s in villages near the Madras border. In 1943–4 peasants were refusing to obey their landlords' orders and to pay taxes and rent; by 1948 up to two hundred villages were claimed as liberated; debts were cancelled, land redistributed, enemies liquidated. Then the army put down the revolt. The Hyderabad peasants seem to have been no worse off economically than those elsewhere and the local social structure was not very different in any major respect. The precipitating factor seems, according to Barrington Moore, to have been the vacillation of the Nizam in attempting to prevent the incorporation of his state into the Indian Union.[8] He had tried to use the communists to buttress his position and it was the temporary weakness of central authority which allowed the communists to establish themselves.

The Latin American states have a longer history of peasant rebellion. Thus Richard Patch describes one immediately ineffective outbreak.

In the large valley of Cochabamba, located in west central Bolivia, with the highest rate of Indian population to arable land, the *campesinos* had long been in contact with the town dwelling *mestizos*. They had become familiar with the norms of *mestizo* culture. As early as 1936, almost immediately after the close of the Chaco war, *campesinos* of one province . . . had established an agrarian 'syndicate' with the aim of freeing themselves from the feudal obligations of service to the latifundium owners and advancing their status towards that of the *mestizo*. The first step was to arrange to lease their holdings from the landlords, thus escaping from the traditional obligations of rendering services to the patron.

Very soon the *campesino* syndicate suffered a setback, which, however, in the long run only served to weld its members more closely into a purposeful and determined group. A number of large landowners of the area banded together to destroy the nascent syndicate and remove this direct threat to the customary pattern of landlord rule. As a first step, in 1939 five landlords purchased those latifundia which the syndicate members had succeeded in renting from the previous owners, took back the lands from the *campesinos*, and cleared large areas by destroying the houses of the *campesinos*. They then proceeded to 'rationalize' the cultivation of the latifundia, retaining the services of those *campesinos* who were willing to become *pegujaleros* [a type of share cropper serf whose obligations differed in minor ways from the older type of *colonos*]. Those *campesinos* who refused to submit were driven from their lands which they and their families had occupied in usufruct all their lives, and often from father to son. This attack upon the syndicate members did more than any other one act to unify the

Indian population and awaken it to political life. Treatment which had hitherto been endured as acts against individual peasants was now recognized for what it was, a concentrated attack by landowners upon the whole group of *campesinos*.[9]

Small wonder, therefore, that governments in India and Latin American states have given land reform a prominent place among promised legislation. For the urban intellectual reform is seen in terms of social justice for the peasant. He is apt to favour forms of corporate farming both as a means of attaining this and also to raise agricultural efficiency. The peasant is far less committed to changes of this order. The economist-planner, endeavouring to raise the productivity of land and/or labour frowns upon the destruction of the highly capitalized plantations or the well-managed latifundium in which agricultural techniques have, for economic or social reasons, been improved; he reacts against the small peasant farmer, with his simple tools and lack of capital and credit. The demands of the peasants themselves are muted; but the threat of widespread rural unrest and even anarchy is a strong stimulus to government action.

In India land reform in the 1950s largely took the form of abolishing some of the intermediaries between the peasant and the state – the absentee landlords and the like, dubbed 'feudal relics' by the Congress party (which they had generally opposed prior to Independence). The benefits to the peasant have, however, been small, for the payments made by him now go to the state. The psychological effects of greater security of tenure are difficult to gauge. The landlords, too, have often defeated the intentions of politicians by cultivating the land themselves and subdividing their estates among family members so that the small farms thus created escape expropriation. In 1959, the Congress party formally adopted a resolution favouring the wide extension of co-operatives, but this has not been implemented. In fact the resolution was the occasion for the creation of the Swatantra party which hoped for the support of the larger peasants. These same groups, dominant in state and local legislatures, have prevented any direct action. The provision of service co-operatives, assisting the peasants in purchasing, marketing and credit, has been a little more successful. But as in Wangala, it is the rich who benefit most. Thus Rosen writes,

97

In fact, there appear to be close relationships among the growth of the new co-operatives, the local political leadership, and the position of the local dominant subcaste. Members of the dominant caste who also hold major political power within the local and state Congress parties have gained by these institutions. They have gained economically by access to credit, fertilizers, seeds and implements; they have gained politically by control of a major source of influence and patronage, and they have gained socially by an improvement in their status as a result of their positions in the new institution. They have at times been able to supplant the old money lenders in money and power. ... The spread of these service institutions has thus been encouraged by the shifting of political power in rural India to a broader group than theretofore; as a result the institutions have been favoured, have grown rapidly, and have been used by the dominant castes and rural groups to expand their output and increase their economic power.[10]

In Bolivia the Movimiento Nacionalista Revolucionario was founded after the Chaco war of 1932 by young officers and liberal intellectuals. It soon absorbed the remnants of a Marxist party and the tin-miners' unions. From 1949 it tried to win peasant support and to control peasant movements, but these tended to develop autonomously. In 1952 the M.N.R. came to power in revolutionary circumstances. Indian miners went into the villages to stimulate the development of syndicates and these the M.N.R. sought to bring within the ambit of the party. But many peasants merely seized the land converting the latifundia into minifundia, and providing food for their families alone, with little surplus to supply the urban populations. Groups within the government debated the form that land reforms should take, and suggestions ranged from the compensation of the landowners to outright expropriation. Ultimately legislation provided for the allocation of land to the poor peasants, the abolition of serf labour, the provision of credit and the restoration, in many areas, of Indian communities. The large estates which were well farmed were protected, though many landowners had fled and the peasants taken over as squatters; others who remained cultivated the land with wage labour. Formal machinery was established to redistribute the land of the traditional estates, but this worked extremely slowly. Work was hampered by lack of maps and surveyors; landowners might, and of course did, appeal at four separate stages in the process. The poor state could not supply the credit sought.

In four years, only 10 per cent of nearly 18,000 estates had been divided by presidential decree – the final step in the distribution process – though in over 10,000 cases a beginning had been made at the lowest levels.

As in India, the Bolivian peasant preferred an individual holding to participation in a co-operative. Here, too, the effect in raising the level of agricultural production was slight. The most noted gains of the reforms seem to lie in the increasing self-assurance of the peasant. The term 'Indian' was officially dropped in favour of 'peasant', peasants began to demand their rights from government officials rather than beg for favours, cap in hand. Other legislation had provided for universal suffrage – prior to 1952, literacy was a qualification for voting.

Peasant rebellions of the type described above are rare in African states for in tribal societies the individual holds his land from a corporate descent group of which he is a member. Even where land is granted to non-members as customary tenants the payments made are usually very small and are seen as denoting the status of the tenant rather than providing a rent for the grantor group. Nevertheless, planners are concerned to find agricultural techniques and land-holding patterns which will raise agricultural productivity. The fact that so little has been achieved in most states is undoubtedly due to the absence of any demand for change from the farmers themselves and to the fact that reforms will bring dislocation to the lives of the farmers without the rewards inherent in the removal of traditional obligations.

Even in the centralized kingdoms the dues paid by the farmer to his administrative overlord – the village and district head – were slight in comparison to the exactions of Indian and Latin American landlords. Nevertheless the ruling aristocracy could be highly unpopular. In Rwanda the transition to parliamentary government in the late 1950s provided the opportunity for the agriculturalist Hutu to overthrow, massacre and expel the Tutsi cattle-keeping rulers (significantly the Hutu movement was strongest in the outlying parts of the kingdom where Tutsi domination was least well developed).

In tribal societies, where landlordism is not an issue, the farmer tends to see the state as the agent of exploitation. Since independence, direct taxes have been increased to pay for education and health facilities; the state has retained, too, a part of the price received for the export crops in the world market. Though undoubtedly benefiting from the improved social services, the farmer has generally not enjoyed a rising standard of living in recent years; he sees the growing affluence in the national capital and argues that the town is exploiting the rural area. The tax riots around Ibadan, cited on the opening pages of this book are one symptom of this discontent; these seem to be but locally organized movements. In Ghana in the mid 1950s, on the other hand, the political leaders in opposition to Nkrumah mobilized the traditional chief of Ashanti and their cocoa-growing rural masses behind the National Liberation Movement, for a while the principal party rivalling the C.P.P.

6   Urban Workers

A poverty-stricken lumpen-proletariat has little revolutionary potential. But on the analogy of western industrial nations, many expect that the urban workers will be in the vanguard of movements of social change; one anticipates a growth of class-consciousness. One of the striking features, however, of life in the cities of the poorer nations of the world is the apparent absence of this phenomenon. Instead one is impressed by the strength of associations based upon ethnic group, home locality and caste. So often the entire social life of the unskilled worker seems to be encapsulated within these primordial groups. This perhaps need not surprise us; but a feature of many of them is the active participation of even the educated men and women of the society. On the one hand these associations serve to facilitate the entry of the migrant into town life; on the other hand they perpetuate traditional values and patterns of behaviour in the urban situation. When violence breaks out in the cities it is more often between ethnic and religious groups than between occupational strata or social classes though economic rivalry may well be the root cause of the conflict.

MIGRANTS

This situation may be a transitory phenomenon. For as we have seen already this century has witnessed the growth of the principal urban centres of the poorer nations at an explosive rate. A twofold growth in three decades can largely be attributed to natural increase, but faster rates are the product of immigration. Thus in Lagos, Nigeria, in 1950 (the date of the last detailed census of that city) just over a third of the population was born in the city; but since a third of the total population was of children under fifteen years of age we may presume that almost four fifths of the adults had migrated to the city. Of these immigrants a third had come from towns and villages in the neighbouring provinces, up to a distance of seventy-five miles; but over a fifth had travelled over four hundred miles from Eastern Nigeria and especially from the over-populated Ibo heartland. As Lagos has continued to grow in the past two decades these figures are not likely to be radically different at the present time.

The cities are thus peopled by men and women who still have close ties to the rural areas. Most return to their homes as often as possible to visit parents and relatives; many are sending home substantial sums of money to maintain the sick and elderly and to educate the young. Most of them will, when asked, state their desire to spend their old age in the place of their birth; in relatively few cases is urban residence seen as permanent. But attitudes among those who are now spending their childhood in the towns is likely to be very different; their ties with an ancestral home which they have visited on but few occasions will be slight. However, as some West African examples show, ethnic associations can still be strongly developed among men who have not only lost contact with their home area but who have also lost their vernacular language in favour of the urban *lingua franca*.

Another feature of these towns which impedes the assimilation of the migrant is the absence, for many, of a stable family life. Approximately half of the Yoruba adult men in Lagos in 1950 were married; and a third of the Ibo. These state figures over-emphasize the case as many of these men will not have reached the expected age of marriage – in fact they may have come to Lagos to earn enough to pay the bride wealth. But many will have left wives and children at home. There is, however, a tendency now for these abnormal sex ratios to decrease. As men expect to spend longer in the town and to see in the town the only hope of gainful employment, so will they bring their families with them.

In the early decades of this migratory process, emphasis was placed on factors which attracted men into the towns. Payments of tax in cash were demanded from farmers who still lived within a largely subsistence economy. Demands for luxury goods were stimulated – the bicycle and sewing-machine for instance – and cash was substituted for foodcrops, livestock and services as a marriage payment. This cash could best be earned in the towns, for save in road or railway construction there were few opportunities for wage employment in the rural area. A high proportion of the migrants were illiterate – schools had scarcely penetrated their home villages. They came to the towns as 'target workers', to earn a specific sum, saving hard and living as cheaply as possible. They stayed for a few weeks or months before returning to their villages; then, in a year or two, they would return to the town to earn more money.

Today the migrants tend to be of a different character. They are being expelled from the villages because of the lack of economic opportunities there. The rising population, changes from corporate to private ownership of farmland, the growing of cash crops both in plantations and by peasants, have reduced the amount of land available to the individual farmer for food crops. The land inherited by a son from his father may well be insufficient to maintain a family. Often this pressure on the land is not directly experienced for the primary-school-leavers have little inclination to farm in the manner of their parents – and no alternative form of agricultural activity seems apparent to them. They therefore move to the town in search of manual or clerical employment appropriate, in their own estimation, to their new qualifications. And from one urban area they move to another.

As an example of this changing trend let us look at Kanpur, in northern India, an industrial town of over 700,000 when it was surveyed in 1954–6.[1] Nearly 70 per cent of the family heads in the city were immigrants and three quarters of these came from rural areas. But the proportion of migrants from urban areas rose from one fifth in the pre-1940 period to one half in the period 1951–5. The proportion who, according to their statements, left the rural area because of insufficient land increased after 1940. Other surveys emphasize the increasing literacy of the migrants. In Gorakhpur, in Uttar Pradesh, only two fifths of the migrants from the rural areas, and less than a fifth from other urban areas were illiterate; one half of the rural migrants and over two thirds of the urban migrants had at least some secondary schooling.[2] In this town the migrants tended to come overwhelmingly from the upper castes; other towns, too, report a significant proportion of educated Brahmins among the migrants.

We stress the lack of opportunity in the rural areas. And so we must emphasize, too, that the migrants are not often from the lowest rural social stratum, forced to emigrate because their lands have been expropriated. They are men who probably have more initiative than their neighbours, and who are prepared to face the risks attendant upon migration in order to strive for economic success and a style of life that is not possible in the rural areas. They come to the towns with hope and with a faith in their own ability. These attitudes may prevail among the migrants in spite of an apparent lack of success. The expectations of the next generation born in the urban slums may be very different.

SLUMS, POVERTY AND UNEMPLOYMENT

The physical appearance of the cities is usually dominated by the affluence and modernity of their centres with their imposing public buildings and multi-storeyed office blocks, and the squalor of most of the suburbs – the shanty-towns. The latter may contain as much as one half of the urban population.

A small Venezuelan *barrio* was described in the following terms:

The barrio of La Laja consists physically of three uneven-shaped blocks of small one-storey houses separated by two wide unpaved streets. . . . Both (streets) are used for parking cars and trucks. . . . As part of the 1962 Community development project trees were planted in these public places. . . . Those who feel inclined sweep the streets, especially the part nearest their houses. City trash collection was introduced . . . and barrels for trash were provided by one of the companies, but this system has not yet completely supplanted the old method of getting rid of trash by throwing it on the beach or in the brush beside the road to the highway. . . . Water is usually turned on for only a few hours in the day; there were often days when no water came at all. Sewage runs off toward river or lagoon in earth channels which in a few places have been lined with cement. . . . Streets other than the two main ones and the entrance road are rough with rocks. All are of earth. . . . Houses in La Laja are constructed of one of the two main building materials: cement blocks or *bahareque*. . . . A *bahareque* house is built by putting up a framework of heavy posts and beams and then tacking thin poles, or more often bamboo, hori-

zontally across the wall area about three inches apart. The wall is then
plastered with a mixture of mud, straw and manure. The most rudi-
mentary version leaves the house at this stage but most houses in La
Laja are then plastered with whitish clay from the river bottom. . . .
There are still eleven houses with thatched roofs. . . . Of the houses in
the barrio . . . less than a quarter were classified as having adequate
outhouses, and over half had none at all. Residents of the latter used
the yard, or more typically the woods . . .[3]

Such squalor derives in part from the rapid growth of the
cities. State and municipal authorities have neither the funds nor
the organization to provide adequate services. In many West
African towns, for instance, there are sufficient enterprising residents to build houses for letting; but elsewhere the migrant sees
no alternative to seizing unoccupied land and erecting a dwelling
out of whatever material is to hand – earth, discarded iron sheets,
packing-cases and the like. He at least may live rent free. But
ultimately of course the squalor is the result of the low income of
the mass of the urban population.

Repeatedly one sees figures showing that up to three quarters
of the urban population is living below the Poverty Datum Line.
Furthermore, many of those in this category are in regular employment. A Nigerian Commission reviewing wages in 1963 con-
cluded 'that a minimum wage should be the level of income
which should be earned by a young unskilled labourer entering
wage employment for the first time and sufficient to meet the
following requirements of himself, a wife and child';[4] here were
listed accommodation (one room), food, according to local diets,
clothing – man: two pairs of shorts, two shirts, one native suit,
one covering cloth, one pair of shoes, and the equivalent for his
wife, transport to and from work and other items – the worker
was allowed two packets of cigarettes a week and three shillings'
worth of drinks. The total for a Lagos worker amounted to £200
a year. But the existing wage rates for unskilled labour in full
employment amounted to less than £100 a year. The Commission admitted that the state could not meet the full increase required and so recommended a substantially lower figure. The
government reduced this figure still further. The Ghanaian census
of 1957 revealed that two thirds of those employed in the public
and private sectors earned less than £120 a year – and this figure

excludes the self-employed and unemployed. Asia and Latin America produce a similar picture of poverty. In the Kanpur survey cited above three fifths of the *households* had incomes below a hundred rupees a month (or less than £100 a year); 19 per cent received between 100 and 200 rupees a month and only 1 per cent above 1,000 rupees.

One is impressed not only by the proportion of urban residents living in poverty but also by the great disparity of incomes between the unskilled labourer and the university graduate. Basically this is determined by the fact that the wages of the farmer are related to the supposed earnings of the average farmer while those of the latter were equated with salaries of men of similar training in western nations. This distinction was institutionalized in colonial Africa. Thus in Nigeria the bureaucracy was divided into a junior and a senior service – the former almost exclusively for Nigerians, the latter for expatriates. The highest possible salaries in the former did not reach the entry point in the latter grade. As Nigerians entered the 'senior service' they acceded to the salaries and perquisites held by the formerly expatriate office holders. The basic system has been perpetuated since Independence with the effect that a primary-school-leaver can expect to earn during his lifetime between £100 and £200 a year; a secondary-school-leaver between £240 and £500; while a university graduate starts at £700 and can rise to £3,000 as a permanent secretary or a university professor. It will be seen that the salary grades do not overlap; advancement to a higher salary is achieved primarily through additional education.

At the present time unemployment in Nigeria among the better educated is only slowly becoming apparent. In India, as we shall see, it has already assumed great proportions; men now take jobs which, a few years ago would not have been thought commensurate with their educational qualifications. Thus some Indian surveys show that the primary-school-educated urban worker earns almost the same as the illiterate; the worker with an incomplete secondary education earns very little more; and the secondary-school matriculate twice as much. This follows the Nigerian situation. But the Indian university graduate teaching in a secondary school usually earns between £250 and £500. While the quality of his education may be lower than that received in African universities, still trying to maintain 'London' standards, the expenditure in time and money in getting a degree is little different.

Income figures alone do not distinguish sufficiently clearly between a privileged category of urban workers who are in permanent employment in the civil service or a large expatriate company and those employed either on a casual basis or by small local entrepreneurs. The former are a privileged group. Most of the better-paid posts are held by them. For skilled and unskilled alike there is much greater security of employment. Health services and facilities for recreation tend to be of a high standard. Formal contracts provide regular holidays. Such jobs are highly prized and once gained are not lightly relinquished. Thus in a study of the large and highly mechanized factory (managed by a subsidiary of the United Africa Company) at Sapele in Nigeria, it was found that under 2 per cent of the workers left annually of their own accord (as against retirement or dismissed).[5] In contrast the turnover of labour was very high in the small Lebanese-owned groundnut crushing mills of Kano; one factory kept only one half of its employees throughout the year, another three quarters. Absenteeism rates were much higher here than in the plywood factory.[5]

Such privileged workers are unlikely to jeopardize their own employment by striking in sympathy with less fortunate workers demanding rights which they, the privileged category, have long since enjoyed. The rising rate of unemployment, particularly among school-leavers, is a perpetual threat to their own security.

In its contribution to the National Development Plan 1962–8, the government of the Western Region of Nigeria stated that the pool of unemployed school-leavers was increasing: it planned to arrest the increase and reduce the pool. In the six-year period it was estimated that 800,000 would leave primary school, having successfully passed the course. Many of these would enter secondary-modern and grammar schools. But the opportunities for employment seemed bleak. Two construction companies in which the government was involved employed one worker: £30 capital; but in ten industrial undertakings the figure was one worker: £4,000 capital. It was anticipated that private investment in the period would amount to £140 million and employ

300,000; government-financed agricultural schemes would absorb over 200,000. But capital expenditure has fallen short of the target while the output of school-leavers continues.

In India the number of unemployed is thought to have risen by 4 million, to a total of over 12 million within the period of the third five-year plan, 1961–6; here, as in other poor countries, the number of new jobs hopefully anticipated by the plans is usually exceeded by the number of new entrants to the labour market. Again, the Kanpur survey gives an example of the nature of the problem. Sixteen per cent of the unemployed were illiterate, 35 per cent had received primary education and 33 per cent had received secondary education; 15 per cent had higher educational qualifications. Over a third of these had been unemployed for more than a year.

Among the illiterates, among those who have had primary education, among the technically trained and the post graduates, the proportions of those who are unemployed for less than a year and those who are out of a job for a longer duration stand in a ratio of two to one. Larger proportions have been unemployed for more than a year among those who have had secondary college education and who by their nature are in a marginal state looking for posts in respect of which they may not stand a fair chance.[6]

As unemployment figures rise so is it seen that the proportion of urban workers employed in tertiary services rises faster than that in secondary or manufacturing industries. In other words, the migrant tries to eke out a living by petty trade or domestic work. Unless an entrepreneurial genius, his chances of a high income are minimal – he is a capitalist without capital, lacking resources both of finance and skill.

Men have migrated to the towns hoping to improve their own living styles and to ensure a better future for their children. They come from traditional societies in which generational differences in wealth could be quite marked. But the occupations open to city-dwellers depend very heavily on educational level. And even though the poorer nations have attempted to increase the opportunities for their citizens these are not equally distributed between rich and poor. Schooling may be heavily subsidized, but the fees may still be beyond the urban worker. Thus the tuition and boarding fees in a Nigerian secondary school amount to about £75 a year – the entire wage of an unskilled labourer. The home environment, lack of books and toys, parents' illiteracy and lack of understanding of the educational system and its values, all contribute to prejudice the chances that a boy from a poor home will pass the entrance examinations. Thus it has been calculated that in both Ghana and the Ivory Coast the son of a clerk or teacher has thirty times as good a chance of entering secondary school as the son of the semi-skilled or unskilled worker; the son of a professional man has well over one hundred times as good a chance. The son of a farmer with perhaps a cocoa farm and a wide network of relatives contributing towards his fees has a higher chance than the urban boy. A substantial proportion of the students now in African universities come from humble homes; but the educated parents have more opportunity to obtain such an education for their children. In the University of Baroda, India, a sample survey revealed that 88 per cent of the students came from the higher castes.[7] Most were from educated homes – in only 37 per cent of the cases did neither parent have secondary-school matriculation, and one third of the families contained a graduate. Eight per cent of the students' families had monthly incomes below 150 rupees (say £120 a year) but a third had incomes above 550 rupees (say £410) – a very small proportion of the total population.

Statistics such as these do not seem to receive wide currency in the countries concerned. The inequality of educational opportunity is not the subject of much discussion in popular newspapers. But slowly the urban workers will come to realize that their social status is to be shared by their children and their grandchildren.

URBAN ASSOCIATIONS

I have so far treated the urban immigrants as statistical categories. But what happens to the migrant, in human terms, when he comes to the city. He becomes 'urbanized' – but what does this mean? To the geographer and economist urbanization is apt to refer to the stabilization of the city's labour force. To the sociologist, however, the term implies an assimilation in the city's culture with the corresponding decline in adherence to traditional rural values and patterns of behaviour. From much writing on this subject, one gains the impression that an impersonal force pervades the city, perhaps like an arc lamp which irradiates the newcomer, the only operative variables being the length of his sojourn in the city and the thickness of his skin – some being more impervious to city influences than others. Sociologists, of course, accept that socialization into new patterns of behaviour is mediated through people, not impersonal forces; but the implication remains that there is a consensus of urban values. Here there is an obvious fallacy, for we read so often of the 'normlessness' and 'anomie' of the rapidly growing city, the lack of well-defined patterns of behaviour. And, as a consequence, there can be no uniform application of sanctions.

Furthermore, a distinction must be made between the internalization of new values and compliance as a matter of convenience. To give a very simple example: the city migrant may arrive on time at his place of work; but on his return to his village this attention to punctuality lapses. Again it is possible to segregate roles in the city: behaviour in the work situation need not be comparable with that in one's leisure hours. To continue our illustration, the punctual clerk or factory-worker arrives an hour late at an evening party, cheerfully claiming that he is observing 'African' or 'Indian' time.

The acceptance of new values and behaviour patterns must be seen therefore not in terms of adaptation to city life in general but to specific situations. In defining the problem in this manner we have shifted the focus of our attention from the city and its institutions to the choices imposed upon the individual resident. In any given situation he has a choice of possible actions, which may range from the more 'traditional' to the more 'modern' with innumerable variants.

Descriptions of the city stress the opportunities open to the migrant, contrasting these with the ascribed nature of much of village life. A wide variety of occupations exist. While associational membership in the village is to a large extent circumscribed by age and descent, the city offers a wide range of voluntary associations. Migration to the city offers a man certain opportunities for social mobility which did not exist in the rural area. Again, in the small rural community, the face-to-face relationships which encompass all the villagers and the multiplex relationships which bind them together make difficult any deviation by the individual from the established norms of behaviour. In fact only by leaving the village can he break free of its constraints. By contrast, in the city the social networks are described as open; one has many friends not necessarily well known to one another. It is easy to reduce the intensity of some relationships or even to sever them completely when these become inconvenient. Thus in manipulating one's personal network of friends, neighbours, relatives and the like one may pursue one's goals, become upwardly mobile, and, in the eyes of many writers, more 'westernized'. Yet when we look at the cities of the poorer nations we find their urban workers so often encapsulated in primordial associations, their behaviour almost as constrained as in the village community.

In emphasizing the opportunities existing in the city writers have under-stressed the factors which limit the choice of the individual migrant. These may best be studied in terms of the resources which he brings with him to the city. He does not arrive in the city as an isolated atom, cut off from his village and without ties in the city; he arrives with a social network consisting largely of kin still in the rural area with a few individuals from that area whom he believes to live in the town. He comes with certain skills, perhaps with some education and literacy in a language other than the vernacular, but probably with no useful technical abilities; these determine the occupations open to him. He comes, in all probability, with little money and is therefore dependent on the generosity of others for board and lodging. He comes, moreover, with a certain mental image of city life which he derived in part from his own family background, in part from the stories of returning migrants.

This last factor is demonstrated very clearly by Philip Mayer in his description of the life of immigrants in East London, South Africa.[8] They are Xhosa from the hinterland of the port and in this rural area Christian missionaries have been active for well over a century. Probably as a result of apartheid the Xhosa have become divided into two social categories – 'School' and 'Red'. The former have accepted Christianity, education and many of the values which we could term 'western' while retaining a rural way of life. The 'Reds' have rejected this completely, emphasizing traditional values and customs. They are termed 'Red' from their continued practice of smearing their bodies with ochre and wearing blankets. When the 'Red' migrant arrives in town

his choices in the matter of forming or maintaining his social network are generally guided by three principles: (1) to keep the relations in good repair, (2) to avoid new ties, especially with non-Red people in town, (3) to show solidarity with the rest of his 'home people' in town. It is from these home people that he chooses his initial host, his room-mates, his regular drinking companions, and his leisure-time associates generally. It is they who are expected to help him in an emergency, to arbitrate in his quarrels and to guide him along the paths of right conduct. These are men related to him by old personalities often existing since boyhood. . . . Hence, the 'Red' migrant relies on 'stretching' his network (geographically) rather than 'enlarging' by working in new acquaintances.[9]

Conversely the school migrant does not emphasize the paramountcy of home ties; 'He tends to build up a new section of network in town, which has no inherent connexion with his old network in the country.'

The 'Red' migrant

will hardly avail himself of the many urban amusements, but will prefer to spend his evenings shut up in a room where he and his friends can drink in 'Red' fashion and 'talk about home'. He will spend little on new clothes or amenities; he may still sleep on the floor, as Red people do in the country. He will cling to pagan religious practices and refuse to be drawn into Christian church activities; he will remain uneducated or semi-educated, or will not learn to read and write solely for practical purposes; he will not aspire to higher education, to white collar jobs, to 'civilization' generally. Twenty or more years in town need not affect this pattern fundamentally.[10]

Although the Red migrant could break out of this pattern his chances are constrained. 'The smarter and more educated people in the town locations evidently do not want a "raw" tribesman as their associate; often enough the church people do not seem to want him much either. If he tries to mingle with them he may meet with rebuffs or insults.'[11] The Red *could* break out but the 'outstanding fact is that according to Red ideas he "ought not" to want to. From childhood he has been taught to despise . . . the learning of town ways, and to regard it as a sign of moral failure only second to . . . absconding'[12] into the town and severing all ties with the home rural area. Thus in East London the dichotomy between Red and School populations is enhanced rather than occluded. But this Xhosa situation seems somewhat unique.

Elsewhere the migrant's anticipation of town life, gained from his home or school experiences, must surely be important; yet it has stimulated little systematic study. The emphasis has been placed upon the dependence of the immigrant upon his urban-based kin, firstly to accommodate him and then to find him a job (and thus relieve themselves of some of their responsibility). The obligations towards the urban kin which thus develop impede any attempts that the migrant might wish to make to sever these relationships. A striking example of such a situation is given in Chinua Achebe's novel *No Longer at Ease*.[13] The hero returns from England where his university education has been financed by his village community. He borrows further from the community to buy a car and so maintain the style of life expected of him. But pressure from the community forces him to reject the girl whom he has fallen in love with and made pregnant because she is an *osu*, a ritual slave, and in the eyes of freeborn Ibo an outcaste.

Relationships between members of a rural community living in the town do not always remain at the impersonal level. Across Africa, and in West Africa in particular, formally organized ethnic associations flourish. In Lima, Peru, very similar associations have been described among the Indian migrants.[14] These associations are based upon quite small communities; among the Ibo of Nigeria they are formed by members of a village if sufficient in number and a village group; Mangin reports that every Peruvian settlement of over a thousand persons seems to have its club in Lima. Membership is voluntary, but in some cases, as among the Ibo, sanctions are so strong that few men refuse to associate with the 'Improvement Union' of their own area. The associations usually have a number of office-holders with titles and roles that are more modern than traditional – president, secretary, treasurer; formal constitutions are drawn up. But the criteria for seniority and office-holding are often a blend of the traditional – descent, age and length of residence, and the modern – educational level.

For the low-paid worker the principal function of the association lies in providing social security – against sickness, death and unemployment. This burden falls not on the nearest kin alone but upon all members through their payment of weekly or monthly dues. The assistance given is of course dependent upon the loyalty of the member in trouble. Secondly the associations provide a source of recreation; and again for the low paid often the sole source, for he is unable to join those associations which demand certain levels of wealth and education, and so serve as indicators of social rank. At the meetings the members discuss the gossip from home, sing vernacular songs and the like.

Members socialize the newcomer to town life, not only helping him to find work but advising him on matters of dress and etiquette. But the association also isolates its members from the town; disputes between members are settled in the meetings according to the perhaps modified norms of the rural community rather than brought before the police and the town courts. Inasmuch as a man's identity in the town is seen largely in terms of his community of origin, so do the urban members endeavour to preserve their own good image by controlling the behaviour of individual deviants. So effective can this be that the number of police needed in immigrant quarters of, say, Nigerian towns is remarkably small.

These associations are however not always concerned only with the lives and affairs of the city migrants; they can be largely instrumental in promoting the development of the rural community. The establishment of dispensaries and schools there is stimulated by the urban association whose members perhaps value these services more highly than the village farmers; individual members can use their influence in government departments to ensure that their community is favoured above others. The extent of such activity will probably depend upon the wealth available from cash crops in the rural area (or remitted by town migrants) and the administrative structure of the state, especially as to the degree to which local development is welcomed. These activities furthermore draw the better educated migrant more closely into the association. Notwithstanding the example from Achebe's novel cited above, they are less dependent upon their own community for social security – they are covered by state schemes for health insurance and pensions, they are least likely, as servants and teachers, to face unemployment. Recreation can be gained from a variety of associations. But not only is pressure brought upon them, by the members of the urban association and by their village kinsmen, to actively assist in the development of the home community, but they see in such tasks an opportunity to gain a personal following which can be used by them to enhance their status and further their interests in the higher strata of society.

The associations include men of all social and occupational categories. For some they come to provide important avenues of social mobility as they seek positions of leadership. For the humble members the association provides a privileged access to professionals from whom they may beg favours or advance their interests.

The role of these associations in facilitating the adaptation of the migrant to urban life has often been stressed. But it is not a 'middle way' which results; rather does it stress traditional values in some of its activities, and more modern values in others. Even within the association the individual has the choice of emphasizing one value or norm over another in furthering his own claims.

Ethnic associations such as we have described in the foregoing paragraphs would seem to fulfil so many functions that we should expect to find them equally developed throughout all cities. However, we find them unevenly distributed. Their weakness or absence in central and southern Africa may be due to the greater paternalism of the mining companies in coping with the problems of their employees. In West Africa these associations are very strongly developed among the Ibo and neighbouring acephalous societies. In these societies a man's status in his village depends upon his descent and age; he loses nothing by absence in the town and is, to this extent, encouraged to retire in and hence to retain close links throughout his life with his home community. Such factors do not operate for the Hausa in Ibadan for example. Here the community is united not by ties with specific Hausa towns, for these seem almost irrelevant, but by adherence to an

Islamic sect – the wealthy entrepreneurs are also the religious leaders. Again, the association of the Mossi from the Upper Volta is strong in Kumasi, Ghana, even among second-generation migrants who have lost contact with their home villages and have become assimilated into the Hausa–Muslim culture of the Zongo. Separate Mossi identity seems to have been stimulated by the government practice, at various periods, of administering through ethnic communities; it is maintained to the extent that certain men see better prospects of attaining positions of leadership through emphasizing Mossi loyalty than through the manipulation of more universal criteria.

In discussing ethnic associations we stressed their role in providing recreation and security for the low-paid urban worker; some associations of this type have developed into para-political bodies capable of exercising strong pressure on governments. These have, of course, a much larger territorial base than the village and are dominated by the more highly educated. Thus at the apex of the myriad of local associations stands the state union, a powerful force in the politics of the erstwhile Eastern Region of Nigeria. But let us examine further the activities of such associations in the Indian rather than the African context.

In the Indian city one might expect that caste distinctions would lose their meaning; the occupations ascribed to particular *jati* are those of the village, not the industrial city. Certainly, within the factory, one does find interaction between individuals which would, in the rural context, flout caste rules. Yet studies show that out of working hours caste members mix almost exclusively with their own group. Thus the Lucknow rickshaw men married within their caste, and dined within the group; their behaviour patterns in their leisure period contrasted markedly with those of working hours. Furthermore, as Sheth's descriptions show, even within the modern factory caste membership can still be significant.

Caste associations in Indian cities are voluntary associations, organized on modern lines; yet as the Rudolphs say in describing them 'the shared sense of culture, character and status tends to create solidarity of a higher order than is usually found among more strictly voluntary associations where a multiplicity of social roles and the plurality of members' values and interests tend to dilute the intensity of commitment and identification'.[15]

The caste associations are formed within the states and bring together members of many *jati* which are of approximately equivalent status. In so doing they provide a valuable integrating function in the state, for unlike the ethnic associations they have no homogenous territorial base which can give rise to secessionist movements. Like the ethnic associations they bring together men of different occupations in the urban sphere and thus constitute vehicles for social mobility and the exercise of leadership.

The energies which the ethnic associations devote to the social and economic development of the home area are, in the case of the caste association, directed towards the raising of the rank of the caste in the local hierarchies. One means by which this is achieved is through sanskritization and the progressive adoption of behaviour patterns of higher castes, so that pollution barriers are eroded. This is a lengthy process but Rudolph describes how the Shanans, toddy palm tappers of Madras, raised themselves during the nineteenth century from the low status ascribed to them and 'breached the pollution barrier, changed their rank within traditional society and (now) occupy an important place in the modern society of Madras and India'.[16] As the foregoing quotation implies the activities of the caste association are equally directed towards obtaining for their members a due share of places in new administrative and educational institutions and a greater political representation. For the lowest castes their associations provide an access to political power which the traditional hierarchy completely denied to them.

Since the caste associations can, or at least claim to, deliver the votes of their members, Indian political parties have tended, on many occasions, to seek caste rather than individual or class support. Thus in Kerala in the 1950s the Communist party relied upon the support of the Irvas and scheduled castes, who comprised a third of the population, the Congress party on that of the Christians and Nairs, and the Muslim league on the Muslims. But here, the fact that the Communists governed in the interests of the poor, and dispossessed, under the banner of class ideology, merely 'crystallised class tendencies within the various communities and helped free their members for mobilization by party rather than community appeals'.[17] Elsewhere the support by ideologically oriented parties for certain castes produced some odd coalitions.

The pattern of caste activity varies from one state to another according to the numerical disposition of the castes and the traditional conflicts between them. Thus low-ranking castes can engage in corporate action to improve their social and economic status. On the other hand a dominant but small land-holding caste can still maintain power by exploiting its vertical relationship with village members. Thus the Reddis of Andhra, though the largest caste in the state, have but 12 per cent of its population. Yet they have dominated the legislatures and most of the political parties. Individual caste members have formed alliances to capture power at different levels but each mobilizes his support within his own community.

Inasmuch as political parties seek popular support through caste associations, they thereby strengthen caste loyalties and allegiances. But as the associations grow in size and in the diversity of economic interests represented, so do factions develop; and as the parties exploit these they emphasize extra caste norms and structures. An example given below is of the Rajputs of Rajasthan. But caste-splits along lines of economic interest are a far cry from the widespread assertion of class-consciousness.

INDUSTRIAL EMPLOYMENT

It might be argued that, in stressing the dependency of the newly arrived urban immigrant upon members of his kin group, home community and caste, and in emphasizing his leisure activities, we have ignored those factors in the urban situation which would encourage the adoption of new norms and values. Thus, it may be claimed, the work situation is dominant in changing men's behaviour patterns. However, such statements tend to be based more on the claimant's basic premises than upon specific research; for very few studies of factory life and organization have been made in the poorer nations. One exception is that of Narayan Sheth; he shows vividly the continuing strength of caste and ethnic relationships even within a progressive and modern Indian factory.[18]

The factory, given the pseudonym 'Oriental', manufactured

power-operated pumps, electric motors and switch-gear equipment. In the mid 1950s it employed almost 900 people. It was located in a town of 300,000 people in Gujarat State. It was an old town which had once been the capital of a small kingdom; its rulers had been progressive since the latter part of the nineteenth century and had actively encouraged the growth of industry. Thus there were in the 1950s over twenty large factories in the city. Oriental was a family-owned firm, but the managing director was also a trained engineer.

Only 14 per cent of the employees at the factory were permanent residents of the town, that is to say men who had forgotten their traditional caste occupation; a further 26 per cent were semi-permanent migrants – men who worked in the city because of their education or skill, but who might well return eventually to their home community. A higher proportion of staff members – 50 per cent – fell into these two categories than workers – 35 per cent. But a substantial number of both staff and workers were classed as temporary migrants or village-based men who moved frequently between city and town. The semi-permanent migrants often visited their home areas, the frequency depending on distance. The Gujarati totalled nearly two thirds of all employees with the Marathi, the next largest ethnic group with 20 per cent, and the Bhaiya with 10 per cent. Few functional units in the factory were dominated exclusively by men of one ethnic group. Nor were the staff predominantly from one group – Gujarati accounted for three quarters and Marathi for 16 per cent. However, a more marked distinction between workers and staff did appear in their caste membership. For 87 per cent of the staff posts were held by men of high and middle caste while these castes accounted for only 46 per cent of the workers. The lower castes predominated in the unskilled jobs. These figures show nevertheless that a significant number of high caste men were in menial jobs even though the higher educational attainments of many of them assured them a staff post.

While on the one hand occupational status in the factory did not follow caste or ethnic lines, ties of kinship and friendship seem to have been an important element in recruitment. A third of the employees had a close relative in the factory and two thirds had a distant relative, caste man or friend. These two proportions are not mutually exclusive; a third of the employees had no link with other members of the factory. Two men seemed to be particularly well placed for getting places in the factory for their kinsmen; of the men interviewed by Sheth 15 per cent were relatives of the managing director (and three quarters of these were staff members) and a third were relatives of the workshop superintendent (one half of whom were workers).

The factory paid good wages. Unskilled workers started at 1 rupee a day; matriculate clerks at 50 rupees monthly, most graduates at 60 rupees; engineering graduates started at 240 rupees monthly. The lower paid workers, however, also received a cost of living allowance of 36 rupees a month, and there were bonuses for full-time attendance. The factory had a good health service. The turnover of workers was relatively low.

The managing director was in effect the representative of the family running the factory and was thus seen by the workers as the symbol of the family.

The relationship of the managing director ... to the employees, was formally a contractional relationship holding as long as the latter were employed in Oriental. However, several employees regarded their relationships with the managing director as a social and religious bond transcending even their present existence.[19]

The term used to describe the managing director, *seth*, likewise implies traditionally a master–servant relationship with social, religious and even fictional kinship ties. Nevertheless, while such terms were used by employees wishing to emphasize their loyalty to the factory, on other occasions the less skilled workers in particular would refer to the management as capitalist and as exploiting the workers. It would be said that the original founder of the factory grew rich from liquor manufacture – an 'unfair' means in the employees' view; that the family ran the factory in such a way as to preserve their personal interests, initially banning trade-union activity. The support given by the managing director to the movement to create a separate Gujarati state was interpreted as an attempt to gain political influence in the local state which could be used to further the exploitation of the workers.

As we have seen caste and ethnic group members were dispersed throughout the factory; and according to Sheth at no time did members of a group combine to further their common interests. But within each unit of the factory interpersonal relationships were seen largely in terms of such group membership. Men abused their fellows in terms of caste and ethnic stereotypes. Men of different groups did not mix much in their leisure periods within the factory. It seems to have been strongly held that promotions were largely determined by caste and kinship ties and not by performance or ability; such allegations, impossible to prove or disprove, would be made by the dissatisfied men. But Sheth shows us too that men who were closely related to those in power in the factory grumbled that they had not been favoured as they had expected.

After a struggle both with the factory management and the state the workers of Oriental organized their own trade union, with 70 per cent of the workers joining. But the participation of the majority was passive and the ineffectivity of the union is ascribed by Sheth to the strong kin ties within the factory and to the relative indifference of the skilled workers – in addition to the management's desire to retain these men, there was a possibility that they might be promoted to staff posts and they therefore emulated the non-unionized staff members.

The picture given by Sheth of informal relationships in Oriental demonstrates the continuing pervasiveness, even within the factory, of caste and ethnic ties and of patronage and nepotism. Yet, as he points out, Oriental is a modern factory and this pattern of relationships, though so contrary to the universalism expected in the West, does not seem to impede the productivity of the factory.

URBAN PROTEST

The dominant theme of a chapter on urban workers must be their poverty – and consequently the desire to ameliorate their own lot and to ensure that their children can exploit more effectively the opportunities which city life seems to offer. How, then, do they articulate their demands? To answer the question one must understand how *they* see the structure of the society in which they live – and their image of it may be very different from ours. Most studies of urban life have given us statistical categories of persons or descriptions of formal associations; there are almost no accounts of the perceptions of city-dwellers of the pattern of social stratification. A brief pilot study which I made among urban workers in Ibadan illustrates such perceptions of one particular ethnic group in one locality. How far it is typical of urban areas elsewhere – and it probably falls nearer to the 'open' society end of the continuum – is a matter for empirical study.

Traditionally, Yoruba society was open. Men from poor homes could, if they had the requisite ability, become very wealthy traders; chieftaincy titles were open to all free-born men and could not be monopolized by a dominant segment of a descent group. But men holding these positions interacted more with members of their descent groups than with each other; they did not constitute a separate sub-culture in the society. Vernacular terms denoted a range of high status positions on the basis of wealth, power and prestige, but none described classes. Even today among English-speaking Yoruba the western class terminology is apt to be misunderstood and misused. In recent decades Yoruba from humble homes have gained education and thus hold well-paid posts in the modern sector of the economy.

On being asked to describe the differences existing within Yoruba society all informants referred to ethnic groupings, distinguishing members of one traditional kingdom from another and, within the town, indigenes from strangers. Differences in wealth and power were seen to be largely determined by fate, though the existence of a patron to give one assistance was strongly emphasized. The need for such a helper was again stressed when the respondent was describing his own aspirations and those which he held for his children – all of which were highly optimistic and, for the poorer respondents, probably fanciful. Respondents tended to accept as fair the wide gap in income between the urban labourer earning £8 a month and the university graduate starting at eight times that figure. The high salary of the latter was justified by the 'suffering' endured in reaching that position through the educational system. To questions on the ways in which they would represent their views to the government most replied in terms of individual lobbying of prominent men while the literates said that they would write letters to the newspapers; none mentioned collective action.

As a result of the nature of the traditional Yoruba society together with the recent experience of the upward social mobility of many into prestigious posts the urban worker in Ibadan sees his society as essentially open though, statistically, his chances of improving his lot are slight. The self-employed craftsman or trader hopes for a lucky break perhaps into some new field of activity; the clerk and teacher see themselves at the base of a career ladder while senior civil servants who see slim promotion chances talk of early retirement and trading. The discordant voices were of factory-workers who found that their occupation gave them little opportunity or incentive for further educational study and little hope of advancement within their factory. But factory-workers do see an avenue for mobility in leaving wage employment and establishing themselves as independent traders or artisans. Though education was recognized as necessary for almost any high position the importance of the patron in helping one up the ladder of success was continually reiterated. Conversely from comments on the desirability of high posts of varying types and on the prestige of different individuals it would seem that many Yoruba value a personal following more than possession of wealth or of administrative responsibility – though these are not mutually exclusive. The emphasis placed upon patronage in facilitating social mobility itself fosters social differentiation in caste and ethnic terms. An appeal to primordial loyalties constitutes one of the most effective means of creating a feeling of obligation on the patron.

Thus achievement and patronage rather than closed social classes and intra-class co-operation still seem to dominate Yoruba thinking. Again, however, one must stress the open character of traditional Yoruba society and how recently people have moved into urban employment of varying kinds; these two factors will not necessarily be replicated throughout the poorer nations.

Many western writers have commented upon the apparent weakness of trade-union activity in the cities of the poorer nations; by implication it *ought* to have been much stronger especially if western industrial nations are taken as the model.

The economic situation of the average worker is pathetic – his wages are low, the gap between his aspirations and the realities of his job is great when he comes to the town. The nationalist fervour which preceded political independence of colonial territories would seem to have provided opportunities for trade unions to show their strength. But they did not usually play a dominant role and their leaders did not attain high political office in the new states. To say this is not to belittle the effects of strikes which have at times nearly paralysed the economy, bringing swift action from government. But the long-term effect of these has been less significant than seemed likely at the time of their occurrence.

A number of factors have been cited to account for trade-union weakness; several of these have already been mentioned *en passant*. First of all, the majority of urban workers are not fully committed to industrial employment; many are first-generation migrants from the rural areas and hope to return there, at least in their old age, and perhaps earlier to resume farming. Men with little skill are apt to change their occupation frequently, from one factory to another and from wage employment to independent occupations in the service or craft sectors. The prestige of self-employment may even cause educated and skilled workers to leave office and factory for trade and professions. Secondly, with high rates of unemployment, the less skilled man does not wish to jeopardize his job either by belonging to a union when this is regarded with disfavour by the management or by participating in a local strike. Conversely the skilled worker, by virtue of his scarcity in most countries, is able to bargain individually with the management for increased status and promotion and may even envisage an opportunity to cross the barrier into the management ranks.

Thirdly, kinship, ethnic and caste associations, both formally and informally organized, can provide much of the social security in these countries that elsewhere would be provided by the state or a trade union. Conversely the strength of the relationships within these associations promotes the reliance upon patronage as a means of advancement rather than collective action.

Fourthly, the relationship between unions and the state is significant. In the less industrially developed states the proportion of workers employed by the government is high. The wage demands made are usually far beyond the ability of government to meet from taxation; government is therefore repressive and may ultimately try to reduce the power of the unions by legislation or intimidation. In the single-party state the government may see the unions as agents of socialization through which the workers might be indoctrinated with the values of the new state and its new élite. The unions become incorporated as one section of the party as happened in Ghana under Nkrumah. Prior to independence the nationalist movements, led predominantly by the western educated élite were, in a sense, competing for the allegiance of the masses with the trade unions and alliances with them were of a transitory nature. For in all poorer nations, and at all periods, one must try to distinguish between collective political action generated largely by the workers themselves and the attempts of rival élite groups to secure the support of the workers, with promises of rewards, in their own competition for political control of the nation.

Lastly, the organization of the trade unions inhibits their effectiveness. Many are organized within a single factory and thus are small, embracing the interests of diverse occupational groups. Union leadership comes, all too often, not from the ranks of the workers but from educated men who have failed to get a government or similar prestigious post; rivalries of many types prevent the development of a unified trade-union structure within the nation, not least of these being the competition between the trade-union federations in the western and communist states for the allegiance of 'third world' unions.

The trade unions are not weak because they have few members – in most countries they embrace a large proportion of those in stable urban employment. They are weak because their members do not choose them as a channel for their demands. (This is a vicious circle – the weaker the union the less members will try to obtain through it.) We have seen that many demands are articulated through patronage relationships. On the other hand the urban poor are often described as being completely apathetic and apolitical. Writers have described how Latin American town-dwellers have shown considerable initiative and organizing ability in seizing unoccupied land in the face of official municipal opposition and developing a new *barrio*. Strong local leaders have emerged. Yet within a few months the organization created has disappeared. One of the most cited reasons for apathy is poverty and the attendant limitations in the social perceptions of the poor – the courses of action which might be open to them. Cited less often is the vulnerability of the poor to sanctions – the fear of unemployment, the activities of the police who continually search in the slums for 'trouble makers' and the lack of support from the better-paid workers when the poorer workers do raise their voices in protest.

The poor often do not see any effective way of influencing government policy; instead of formulating demands, for example, for higher wages, they protest when the government imposes austerity measures; they seek short-term goals, often supporting an essentially conservative politician who promises them work rather than a radical one who seeks to change the structure of society. Typically, frustration is seen as leading to violence. But violence is not the prerogative of the poorer urban workers.

Calcutta has a reputation of being one of the most violent of Indian cities. According to Myron Weiner

Demonstrators come from many social classes, but those demonstrations in which the middle classes form the core are most likely to be violent. The 1943 famine, which impoverished the Bengal countryside and killed hundreds of thousands of villagers, resulted in little violence. Working-class strikes in Calcutta only rarely involve violence and almost never involve the entire city; and the many refugee agitations held in Calcutta have remained largely non-violent. In contrast, the violent agitations in Calcutta have been those involving the middle class: the strike against an increase in train fares, the strike for an increase in teachers' salaries, and a small but violent agitation in 1954 of orthodox Hindus calling for a government ban on the slaughter of cows.[20]

The causes are difficult to ascertain. Police ineptitude and misjudgment often trigger off the violence. Professional rowdies exploit it – they are thieves of many kinds, long-time urbandwellers who have severed their links with their rural origins. The middle occupational groups *do* belong to trade unions and political parties; pressure groups do lobby the political leaders. Weiner argues that many Calcutta citizens, particularly members of the middle classes, turn to coercive and sometimes violent methods in their attempts to reach the government in the belief that only through such coercion is it possible to obtain government help or to prevent the government from making an unpopular decision. There are many reasons for this great distrust of authority, not the least important being that government officials are in fact unresponsive to many of the demands made by the urban middle classes.[21]

Civic affairs are largely the responsibility of the government, which ought therefore to provide more services for its citizens. But those in power are largely corrupt – and any who might replace them would be equally so. Since rational efforts to influence the government rarely succeed, violence is seen by the citizens as their most effective instrument.

7   The Men at the Top

In the previous two chapters we have seen how villagers have exploited new economic opportunities, raising living standards and slowly changing the rural social structure. But peasant protest movements are rare in the poorer nations and when they do occur are as apt as not to be conservative in their goals or perhaps dominated by fantasy. Men have flocked to the rapidly growing towns to seek work; many remain unemployed for long periods; many, too, work spasmodically for low wages. The incomes of most are well below what is judged to be a minimum to adequately feed, house and clothe a small family. Yet the trade unions, through which the workers might be expected to voice their grievances, are poorly organized and relatively weak. Often the aspiration levels of the workers remain high and they look to relationships of patronage to provide them with opportunities for self-advancement. The dominant associations for many workers are those based upon ethnic group, village of origin or caste.

THE COMPOSITION OF THE ELITE

The future of the poorer nations rests with a very small minority holding positions of power in the political parties, in the civil services and in business. This, of course, is so in any country. But the poor articulation of interests among the farmers and urban workers gives this élite added power; they can manipulate the masses rather than accede to their demands. Very loosely we may term those men at the top the western educated élite. For, in achieving high-ranking positions in government or business, a western-style education has almost invariably been a prerequisite. The secondary schools of our non-African and Asian colonies resembled the English public school both in their structure and their curriculum; in the French colonies the ties with the educational system of the metropolitan country were even closer. Many of the élite of the poorer nations have in fact been educated in universities in western Europe and the United States. By their education these men have come to adopt substantially western styles of living; they feel that, in their own country, they are entitled to salaries commensurate with those of their European or American classmates who remained in their own countries. A vast gulf, both in culture and in mode of life, thus separates the western educated élite from the masses.

Sometimes the members of this élite are termed intellectuals, a term which would emphasize their educational superiority and their initiative in the innovation of new values. In our own society, however, we usually think of the intellectual as marginal to the government and business establishment; he is the freelance writer or a university teacher. In the poorer nations many of the outstanding scholars are indeed in university posts; but many too are in political parties or the civil service. The three Nigerian novelists who first found fame – Chinua Achebe, Cyprian Ekwensi and Timothy Aluko – have all held very senior civil service posts; Senegal's philosopher-poet, Leopold Senghor, is also her president and creator of the dominant political party.

The members of these western educated élites are innovators; they have been most successful in exploiting the new opportunities which have been created as their countries have been drawn further into the world economy and the global political field. The question that we must ask is: from what social groups have those men emerged? Are they from the families of traditional rulers or landed aristocrats or have they risen from humble rural homes? What interests do they represent over and above their own personal status? Furthermore, is the composition of the élite changing; are the new recruits being drawn from a social stratum different from that of earlier generations. In describing traditional societies we saw that a high rate of social mobility often existed; even within peasant communities the distribution of wealth between families could fluctuate widely over generations. Yet inasmuch as the highly educated men in the élite have reached this status mainly through their own ability (and not through their parents' wealth) and tend to marry wives of similar ability, we might expect their children to have considerable innate ability. Added to this factor is the great difference in home environment between that of the élite families and that of the urban worker or farmer. The élite can ensure a high measure of educational success for their own children while, as we have already seen, the children of the urban poor have but a minimal chance of entering a secondary school. A modern society in which the high-ranking positions are allocated on the basis of education may be more open than a traditional one in which political office, and thereby wealth, is reserved for members of a few families; but it may be considerably less open than many of the pre-colonial societies of Africa and Asia.

The composition of the élite, both its western educated and traditional elements, in any one country is a matter for empirical study. The variety in the patterns is large. Here we can but illustrate it with reference to a few countries in Africa, Asia and South America. Many writers have referred to the substantial homogeneity within the élite of any one country – its members are of the same social origin and have similar styles of living. The contrast is drawn with the more diversified élite of the industrial nations. Yet the principal theme of this chapter is the competition for power, wealth and prestige between the categories and groups which compose the élite. This competition provides the mainspring of much of the political activity of the state. Individually and collectively men aspire to the highest ranks in the stratification systems and, having achieved these, endeavour to maintain the values (or the rules for advancement) on which their success is based. Others challenge these values hoping thereby to enhance their own positions. To an increasing degree these struggles are not confined within the élite. Political domination must be legitimated, both in the sight of the world at large which expects political leaders to be representatives of their people, and at home where peace rests upon the acquiescence of the masses. Furthermore, a political party or group which seeks to effect radical changes in the structure of society must mobilize the masses into a more active support of its cause. In their struggles the competitors within the élite seek the support of the masses, or at least of specific categories. The manner in which they do this is conditioned to a large degree by the social distance which separates them.

Africa

First let us look at the composition of the élite in the newly independent states of Africa, taking our examples from Nigeria and Ghana.

The élites of these territories, in the pre-colonial period, were the traditional rulers of the many kingdoms and chiefdoms, together with wealthy traders, and in many societies, ritual specialists who enjoyed high prestige and perhaps considerable power though they retained a modest style of life. British administrative policy maintained the kings and chiefs as agents of local administration, and inasmuch as these offices remained powerful, men with primary and secondary education were, in the later colonial period, attracted to them. Yet the influence of these men has remained largely confined to their areas of traditional jurisdiction and they have gained very little influence nationally. The prime exception to this generalization are the emirs of the Hausa–Fulani states of northern Nigeria who probably increased their power during the colonial period and were a dominant force in the Northern People's Congress, the party which formed the government of northern Nigeria and was the senior partner in the Federal coalition. Opportunities for trading in the traditional manner were increased in the colonial period with the marketing of cash crops – cocoa, palm products, groundnuts – and the provision of lorry transport. Yet even though they tend to have little education, the influence of these traders does not go far beyond their home areas. To the extent that most men and women now profess Christian or Muslim values and beliefs, the influence of traditional ritual specialists is now negligible.

In the absence, save in the case mentioned above, of a traditional élite which retains substantial power, the national élites of Nigeria and Ghana are western educated. In Ghana the first men to receive education came from trading families living near the coastal forts of the European powers; in Nigeria the freed slaves who had returned from Sierra Leone in the middle of the nineteenth century and settled in Lagos were also evangelists for Christian mission teaching and education. During this century a few Africans rose to high offices both in the churches and in colonial administration. But this process was then halted and Africans found their only outlet in the private professions, and especially in medicine and law. The educated nineteenth-century West African first sought acceptance on terms of equality by the coastal European society; it was only when he felt rejected that he tried, in many cases, to re-establish his links with African society. These few highly westernized families tended to invest their savings in landed property and, from its income, to provide for the education of their children and grandchildren who are, therefore, still largely within the present-day élite. But they are now numerically insignificant in the vast number of secondary-school-leavers and university graduates produced in the past two and a half decades.

During the colonial period primary education was directed towards the production of teachers and of clerks for the 'junior service' of the colonial administration. Chiefs and wealthy traders obviously had the financial resources to pay for education for their sons; but in many areas they were reluctant to send the boys to mission schools in which proselytization was marked, and the often explicit instructions to flout traditional norms alienated the sons from their families and often brought disgrace to their elders. In contrast, men of humble status had less to lose; in fact the prestige of an educated son outweighed any honour for which they might strive in the traditional society. A few secondary schools were maintained by the government and missionary bodies but few of their products went further for a university education. Thus in the early 1920s Nigeria had only thirty graduates (including fifteen lawyers and thirteen doctors and mostly resident in Lagos). In 1945 less than two hundred Nigerians were pursuing studies of any kind in England. The rapid expansion of education dates from the immediate post-war period and the ensuing decade. Universities were opened in Accra and Ibadan and more scholarships were provided for overseas study. Today, over a thousand Nigerians graduate annually from local universities alone.

We have already stressed the manner in which educated

parents endeavour to obtain for their children at least as good a training as they had enjoyed. We have seen that the son of a professional man has a far better chance of entering secondary school than the son of the urban labourer. Yet so rapid has been the expansion of higher education in West Africa that one finds that the rising élite is being recruited to a high degree from humble homes. Thus, of a sample of Yoruba university graduates resident in Ibadan in the early 1960s, one third had fathers with little or no primary schooling and only one third had fathers who had received post-primary education. Similarly in the University of Ghana in the early 1950s a quarter of the students came from farming families – though almost as many were from professional homes.

Africanization of the public services began in earnest in the early 1950s and Nigerians and Ghanaians acceded to the salaries and perquisites of the expatriates whom they displaced and supplemented. Only slowly have some of the privileges relating to overseas leave been whittled down. Thus the Nigerian university graduate usually earns at least £700 a year initially and can rise by increments to nearly £3,000 in the most senior civil service posts. It might be argued that these men, who so often have come from humble homes, could well live in a style closer to that of their parents. However, though Africans have now largely replaced expatriates in all permanent posts in the public service, the number of expatriates in these countries continues to increase, the newcomers being advisers in development, businessmen and the like. So, in Nigeria in the early 1960s of persons employed in the senior category (university graduates and persons with similar professional skills and qualifications) 24,000 were Nigerians, 8,000 were expatriates. The educational qualifications of the latter are equalled by many Nigerians, but the expatriates tend to receive much larger salaries to compensate them for their contract status and life abroad. These expatriates maintain a style of life that the African envies even though he may not wish to emulate it in every detail.

A corollary of the low level of African economic development in the pre-colonial period is the present state control of most public services and utilities. Add to this the weakness of the secondary-manufacturing-sector of industry and one will appreciate that a very high proportion of the educated men of the African state are employed in the public sector. In Ghana, for instance, four fifths of the western educated professionals are employed in the public sector compared with 11 per cent in the private sector and 4 per cent self-employed. One half of those classified as administrators are in public employment.

Expatriate companies in Nigeria and Ghana have been anxious to employ West Africans in top positions, partly for economic reasons and partly to improve the public image of the company. But the incentives and opportunities for the well-educated African to enter the field of business on his own are limited. He lacks capital, the small family savings probably having been exhausted in his own education; he seeks immediate rewards, partly in order to finance the schooling of relatives and so repay his debts. The business community is thus still largely dominated by the managerial staff of the expatriate companies – and most of the key positions continue to be held by expatriates.

Members of the Nigerian or Ghanaian educated élite enjoy styles of life which are narrow in range. They come from similar backgrounds, they have been to the same few secondary schools and universities; they are in similar types of employment – civil servants, professionals, managers. Many live in houses originally built for expatriates; the range of furnishing material available in the local shops is limited. They are a small and cohesive group living predominantly in the national or regional capitals, in government residential areas or élite suburbs. Friendship patterns link men and women of similar income and one does not, in Ibadan for instance, find any marked segregation of those in the civil service, the university or the self-employed. A number of formal associations – the major charities, rotary club, old boys' societies – are restricted to members of the élite.

This educated élite is composed largely of young people; in Ghana, in 1960, one half of the well-educated professionals and administrators were under thirty-five years of age. Most of these young men have parents and siblings still living in their rural homes or in the older quarters of the towns. They visit these relatives frequently and, as we have already seen, spend a substantial proportion of their salaries in paying for the education of their junior kin. It is a duty incumbent upon any man who has achieved élite status to raise as many others from his immediate family as he can. The educated man is expected furthermore to take an active part in the affairs of his home community, being called upon to give his advice and to use his influence in matters such as the building of a new school. In the city, he will be expected to be active in the affairs of his town or village ethnic association, and to seek employment opportunities for the recently arrived immigrant. These are obligations which the educated man may avoid – but only at the cost of losing the support of members of his kin and community. Furthermore members of the élite may themselves accept that they ought to be active in the affairs of their community and will esteem those who are, and denigrate those who are not.

I have written so far exclusively of the most highly educated men, who in consequence occupy the top posts in government and business. Below them rank the sub élite or 'middle class' of clerks, teachers, small traders and the like. Broadly, these men have a humble social origin similar to that of most of the élite. They are the less fortunate ones who dropped out of school because of their limited academic ability or because they could not find the fees. Many of these continue to study privately hoping thereby to re-enter some institution of higher learning and gain further academic qualifications which will be matched by the appropriate increments. They cherish their relationship with kin and friends who have achieved success and are in a position to promote their own advancement. But the great difference in income achieved through three years of university education – raising a man from £240 a year to £700 – is of course reflected in the very different styles of life enjoyed by these two categories.

India

The composition of the Indian élite resembles in many respects that of African states, the corollary of a common colonial experience. But in several important respects there are marked differences. India has a longer history of secondary and university education and, as a result, a larger number of families who have accepted western values over several generations. She has more locally owned industry and hence a significant business élite. Western education was embraced by the Brahmins and the upper castes have retained their superiority in the modern sectors; contrast the African situation where the educated have generally been drawn from all social strata. Finally, the traditional culture of India, because it traversed the sub-continent and was not exclusively based upon village deities and ancestors, has retained its vigour and there is a sharper dichotomy between the westernized and traditional styles of life. Let us look at these points in more detail. The leading Indian secondary schools date from the early years of the nineteenth century. These were usually modelled on English public schools; fees are high – as much, often as the annual income of a lecturer in a good university. Those who attend such schools tend to be highly conscious of their exclusive status. In 1857 the universities of Bombay, Madras and Calcutta were founded, though as examining bodies for local colleges and not as corporate bodies. The prestige of graduation from a foreign university and especially from Oxford or Cambridge remained high. It was from these people, enjoying such educational privileges, that most of the early leaders of the Congress party came; Jawaharlal Nehru, a Brahmin, son of one of India's most successful lawyers, was educated at Harrow and Cambridge, and epitomized this category, and stands in marked contrast with later leaders such as Lal Bahadur Shastri – son of a poor schoolteacher, never seen in western clothes and ill-at-ease in the western idiom, who had not travelled outside India before becoming Prime Minister.

Brahmins and other high-caste men dominated the early educated élite and have continued to be prominent in schools and colleges. In the early years of this century, Indian entrants to the Indian Civil Service in Madras and Bengal, for example, were almost exclusively Brahmins. The values placed by the caste on learning facilitated the transition to the new medium. But of course only a very small minority of the Brahmins could exploit this new opportunity; many are still peasants or, as the composition of the labour force at the 'Oriental' factory has demonstrated, have become manual labourers.

The composition of the Indian Administrative Service, heir to the Indian Civil Service, illustrates the hereditary factor in the composition of the highly educated élite. The service now numbers about 2,000 men who are attached to the civil services in the constituent states, only half of them serving in their native state. Most of them are recruited by examination, the number of entrants usually being twenty times those selected. Of entrants in the years 1948–62, 44 per cent were sons of men employed in government service; 14 per cent were sons of professionals – doctors and lawyers; 13 per cent sons of teachers and 10 per cent sons of businessmen. The parents of a third of them earned more than 900 rupees a month (or £800 a year) – the salary of a member of the I.A.S in the senior grade; parents of a further half earned between 300 and 900 rupees a month – the salary range of an I.A.S. civil servant of junior grade, or of the more highly-paid secondary-school teachers. The number of entrants from poor homes did in fact double during this period; the explanation given is that while the poor were assisted by scholarships and by the reservation of places for members of the scheduled castes, the middle classes had less to spend on education if they tried to maintain, in an inflationary period, their former style of life.[1]

While India has developed this modern-oriented educated élite, the traditional rulers, the rajahs and princes, remain influential and wealthy. Basically their political power was withdrawn with the institution of a republican constitution at the national and state levels following independence in 1947. But their loss of income from traditional sources was replaced by government subsidies. These are most jealously guarded by the rulers who have acted collectively to maintain and even to increase their allowances. The government, though increasingly dedicated to socialist principles, for long felt unable to abolish this relic of a 'feudal' period for fear of unpopularity in provincial towns and villages.

The fate of one traditional group has been graphically described by the Rudolphs.[2] The Rajputs, a warrior caste, were the rulers of more than twenty kingdoms which were merged into the new state of Rajasthan; they were reared on values of loyalty and valour and saw commerce and intellectual pursuits as degrading. In the new state their rights to land were preserved; landlords continued to hold one half of the productive land, much of which was held as fiefs by the kin and followers of the princely families. But when those Rajputs who had been displaced from traditional palace duties tried to return to their land and evict their tenants, they were prevented by the government. These men fell to the status of peasants or lower. The more affluent had sufficient resources to maintain their status, yet the projected land reforms threatened them too. They had formed a caste association well before independence and this was controlled by the biggest landlords. In the 1952 election the Rajput party won only one seat less than the Congress party which thence sought its support. The reforms proposed favoured the larger landowners bearing hardly on the small ones; the latter seized control of the caste association and emphasizing the traditional ethnic called on the caste to defend its rights. In 1954 the association mobilized its members into passive resistance in the streets and hunger strikes. Land reform thus split the caste, the wealthier members allying with the Congress party, the poorer becoming a traditionally oriented opposition group, prone to violence.

While the higher ranks of the civil service and of the major political parties are occupied by the western educated élite, at the local level the traditional élite are still largely dominant. Thus Brass writes of Uttar Pradesh,

In all four rural districts studied, the leadership and the major sources of support for the local Congress organizations have been drawn from the high caste ex-tenants of the *zamindars* and *talukdars* and from the petty and middle ex-*zamindars*. Power in the countryside rests upon the control of the land. The power of the Congress rests upon its network of relationships – established through its leadership and through its control of local government and co-operative institutions – with the locally influential communities in the villages, with those who control the land.[3]

This local élite differs from that which predominates in most African states in that it is far less influenced by western education (in India English is not usually taught in the primary schools). It is, through its control of land, far more powerful; and furthermore, inasmuch as this control is now threatened, it is apt to emphasize traditional values which supported its claims and thus became an ultra-conservative group; the poorer Rajputs described above are a clear example of this tendency.

It is sometimes asserted that India lacks a business élite – a bourgeoisie 'exerting the kind of pervasive social and political influence which is apparent in the Western societies'.[4] As in Africa, the products of the schools turned to the professions; traditional crafts and village industries were killed by the competition of exports from the industrial West. But members of certain castes, traditionally noted for their commercial activities, have turned to manufacturing industry, banking and the like. The owners of the 'Oriental' factory cited in the previous chapter are an example. These men were not active in the nationalist movement before independence; but they did subscribe heavily to the funds of the Congress party. Both before and after Independence they would lobby the government, and with considerable success, only when issues arose which specifically concerned them. They seem to have remained unperturbed by the Congress ideologies of socialism and village development; any form of rapid economic development would benefit them and a popular and stable government would encourage private investment. However in 1959 the Swatantra (Freedom) Party was founded, to promote the claims of the private entrepreneur; it opposed proposals for joint farming and for ceilings on land-holdings as well as further nationalization and the imposition of controls on business. It favoured a greater role for the private sector, emphasizing a nineteenth-century ethic of free enterprise.

We have already mentioned the high rate of unemployment among educated Indians as youths leave secondary school and university and wait for years to gain a job which they feel appropriate to their qualifications. We have also seen how the poorer members of traditional local élite groups have suffered as a result of land reforms. The frustrations of those aspiring to higher status and the anxiety of the displaced, make these 'middle classes' most prone to violence as the examples of the Rajputs and of the Calcutta riots have already demonstrated.

South America

The traditional élite of South American states such as Peru or Colombia was, of course, western educated; for it derived ultimately from the Spanish conquerors. This élite retains its superior position today. While some writers have emphasized its changing character, others stress the degree to which the élite has maintained itself during half a century of rapid political and economic change. The two viewpoints are complementary, not incompatible.

In Colombia and some of the neighbouring states the élite is popularly termed the oligarchy, society being divided into this group and the masses. Basically it derives its status from the ownership of land. Four per cent of Colombia's farms account for two thirds of the cultivable land of the country and the owners of these *hacienda* are the core of the élite. They live not on their estates but in the provincial and national capitals, a distinct sub-cultural group. A noble ancestry is important; in Popayan, a rather conservative town, the élite families have their armorial bearings carved over their front-doors. However, élite status rests not only on ancestry – one must also have the wealth necessary to maintain the social position. The oligarchy is essentially white and though most families must contain at least a small proportion of Indian blood, they pride themselves on their 'racial' purity. Intermarriage within the oligarchy is the rule and this promotes a distinctive style of life, emphasizing leisure and cultural pursuits and standing in marked contrast to the style of the *mestizos*, let alone the Indians. Education was the prerogative of the oligarchy; it is only in the recent decades of this century that secondary schooling has been widely available to the masses. A sample of students at the National University in Bogota in 1961 reported their social class origins to be as follows: lower or lower middle, 5·4 per cent; middle, 80·3 per cent; upper middle, 7·6 per cent; upper, 6·7 per cent. Many of the 'middle class' students are upwardly mobile, but the figures do emphasize the relatively high proportion of students from élite families, and the few who came from the masses.[5] The oligarchy has always sought a professional training for its sons, seeing this as befitting a gentleman landowner.

The traditional oligarchy dominated all spheres of activity – government, education, the professions and business. It has been termed a network of families controlling wealth. Substantial power rested with family heads who could place their kinsmen in strategic positions. The individual was highly dependent upon his patron, overtly obsequious towards him but also liable to stab him in the back if he failed in his supposed obligations.

Traditionally, members of the oligarchy did not look upon entrepreneurial activities with great favour. As a consequence many of the opportunities created in the present century have been seized by self-made men rising from artisan elements in the middle class or by immigrants from abroad. These have perhaps moved into the families of the landed gentry and now claim élite status – a claim often repudiated by both the gentry and those ranked immediately below the *nouveaux riches*. Some have purchased their own *haciendas*. But in Colombia the extended families of the élite have often moved into commerce or industry while retaining their rural ties. Sons of the gentry have returned to their estates and, with capital gained in urban activities, have raised the productivity of the land. In Peru, comments Bourricaud, the oligarchy did not venture into enterprises carrying substantial risks.[6] Thus it was small men who stated the fish flour industry and then, as competition developed, the financiers intervened to control and rationalize the industry. As Dix reports for Colombia, economic power in these states tends to be highly centralized. Seven large industrial firms held 30 per cent of the capital in manufacturing enterprises held by Colombian nationals.[7] Whatever their ancestry Colombian business leaders are well educated; over half the owners and managers of large businesses in Bogota had attended a university and only 6 per cent had not completed their secondary education. Furthermore the élite of these states has actively co-operated with foreign industrial interests.

Just as the élite has been open to recruits from the more skilled and educated of the masses and from immigrant populations, so have some of its own members fallen in occupational status. One reason is that élite families tend to be large and have relatively low rates of infant mortality; the oligarchy cannot support them all. The 'middle class', so termed, in Colombia thus consists of two categories. The traditional middle class comprises professionals, bureaucrats, medium landowners. Many of its members are impoverished descendants of great families; they still try to emulate élite behaviour patterns. They tend to be even more conservative than the élite itself. On the other hand there is a new middle class of small shopkeepers, artisans, lower level bureaucrats with incomes perhaps little different from those of many of the traditional middle class. The new middle class is derived from upwardly mobile rural immigrants, less white than the traditional middle class. It is more interested in money, less in culture and tends to political non-conformity. The distinction between these two categories though far less easy to define in specific situations than to enunciate in general terms, seems an important factor in political activity in these countries. As each category has interpreted social change in its own way, and as each tends to identify, though for different reasons, with the oligarchy, the middle classes have not evolved as a political force. It has been termed apolitical. As one critic wrote, 'The Colombian middle class acts neither as a liberalizing nor a stabilizing element in the nation's social struggle. It has gained no political competence of its own, for it has traditionally equated its interests with those of the oligarchy. In a general way, its function has been to sharpen the conflict by tending to increase the numerical strength of the "enemies" of the masses.'[8] Yet Dix argues that this middle class is becoming more self-conscious, forming associations to protect its interests and being specifically wooed by politicians. The élite could well grant the middle strata a larger share of political leadership without endangering its own status. But if the middle strata are to wage an effective political battle for their interests they will need to ally with other groups. The question is, which?

INTRA-ELITE CONFLICTS

In describing the composition of the élites of the poorer nations we have stressed, and especially in respect of Latin America and Africa, their homogeneity. In the western nations we tend to speak of a plurality of élites – political, business, intellectual, trade union, military, etc. – each with a distinctive style of life and social origin. Yet we have asserted that competition within the élite provides in the poorer nations, the mainspring of political activity. Where then, do the divisions lie?

In Colombia the Conservative and Liberal parties have alternated in power for a century. They appear to have the framework of modern parties. Yet they are in fact based upon factions within the oligarchy – divisions which have been termed 'hereditary hatreds'. Within the oligarchy, party allegiance is virtually ascribed by one's birth; and since the extended family may embrace a wide number of interests – landowning, business, professional, etc. – so the party cannot be defined in terms of any specific grouping of interests. Furthermore the allegiances of the élite are assumed by the tenants on their estates and by others through relationships of clientage. In fact whole villages are identified as adhering to one party or the other. And at the rural level the vehemence with which political contests are fought greatly exceeds that of the capital. Such loyalties, based upon patron–client relationships, have militated against the development of peasant consciousness.

Even though one cannot define the parties in terms of interest groups, the Conservatives and Liberals have espoused ideologies which reflect their respective labels. The Conservatives stress order and hierarchy, the Liberals, liberty and popular rule. In recent years the urban areas have become Liberal strongholds and this cannot be attributed solely to the greater immigration of Liberals who suffered persecution in their home villages; many men must have changed their political allegiance in the town. To many immigrants the Liberal party is seen as the party of the urban workers, while the Conservatives were as a corollary identified with the landed interests. Thus in the urban situation class identification was being imposed on the parties, not by the élite but by the masses.

A ruling élite is concerned to maintain the structure of society and its own privileged position within it; specifically it endeavours to uphold the rules by which positions of wealth, power and prestige are allocated. In the poorer nations the interests of the élite are, in this century, being threatened to an ever-increasing degree. Traditional rulers have been supplanted by popularly elected parliaments though many still retain considerable local influence and prestige, landowners are threatened as politicians try to meet the demands of the peasants by measures of land reform. Businessmen are threatened when the politicians look to increased state control of industry as a means of speeding the rate of economic development. In these circumstances men with common interests tend to combine in an effort to stem the encroachments upon their privileges. And since they are numerically small categories they have to seek outside support, mobilizing it perhaps in terms only indirectly related to their own interests. Thus the wealthy Rajput landowners formed a caste association and the Indian businessmen the Swatantra party which appealed to the rich peasant as well as to the industrialist. But landowners or businessmen are themselves not necessarily homogeneous categories; the example of the Rajputs illustrates the division between the rich and poor landowners and the subsequent rift in the caste association. Similarly the interests of the larger businessmen who are closely connected to expatriate firms diverge from those of the small entrepreneur who seeks protection from foreign competition.

Thus while the interests of the élite are becoming more openly articulated through political parties, divisions within the various categories inhibit the identification of a single broad interest with any one party. Similarly, as parties in opposition seek support from a variety of disgruntled interest groups, so do they fail to become identified with any major category of persons.

The discussion so far of the divisions within the élite seems inapplicable to Africa where the élite is both too recent in origin to have developed the factionalism described in Colombia and usually lacks among its members businessmen and landowners. But are the African élites so homogeneous?

The western educated élite occupies a highly privileged position in terms of the style of life which it enjoys. It certainly seeks to maintain this position and suggestions that civil servants and men similarly employed should receive substantial cuts in their salaries are quickly and quietly disposed of. Yet those privileges do not arouse the hostility of the masses largely because the high incomes are seen as the due rewards for ability and effort in passing examinations and because these incomes are used in part to raise the status of other family members. Divisions within the African élite derive, in the first instance, from the competition for high office within the growing machine of government. In the private, as well as in the public, sector educational attainments are a prime determinant of one's career prospects. In fact, to most men, education is seen as virtually the sole criterion of achievement, and hostility is expressed towards those who reach the top by other routes. Thus, although many of the leading politicians are well-educated men – teachers, doctors and lawyers for instance – others have risen through the hierarchy of the party organization after dropping out of school. Senior civil servants do not like to be overruled by ministers who are educationally inferior. Again within the civil service promotion still tends to be made on the bases of age and seniority; but with the recent rapid expansion of higher education and the civil service, recent entrants with doctorates are uncomfortably inferior to seniors with mere pass degrees. The competition for promotion in periods of rapid expansion of the public services, and for initial appointment as this expansion ceases while the supply of graduates continues to increase, encourages men to seek their personal advancement through patronage, and especially through men of their own locality or ethnic group upon whom the obligation to help is strongest. Conversely frustrations are expressed in terms of ethnic favouritism. These tendencies are exacerbated by the participation of the élite in the affairs of their own home communities both through their kin ties and through ethnic associations and also by the interpretation of differences in educational attainment between ethnic groups as an attempt by the more advanced group to dominate the others. We shall examine a situation of this nature in the next chapter in discussing the Nigerian civil war.

One would readily expect that a ruling élite of businessmen or landowners would be concerned primarily to preserve the bases of their economic power and would oppose major structural changes in their society. By the same token one would probably expect that a ruling élite composed largely of intellectuals would be far more radical. It is true that the leaders of revolutionary movements have been drawn primarily from this category – yet the present rulers of so many post-colonial states of Africa and Asia seem essentially conservative. Why should this be so? By their education the intellectuals have cast off many of the traditional modes of thought and have experienced a perhaps bewildering variety of new ideas. As civil servants or professionals they are virtually assured of a privileged role in society whatever its structure, whether it be capitalist or socialist. Yet it is not so much their position relative to that of others in society which they seek to preserve but their actual privileges – the style of living which in the past decade or two, they have come to enjoy. In material terms this is a western or international style and the educated African, for instance, expects a standard of living commensurate with that of expatriates of similar education and experience – and especially so when large numbers of expatriates still live in the major cities.

The western educated élite is usually dedicated to rapid economic development; this is not likely, of itself, to threaten its own status, as it may well threaten the status of indigenous businessmen and landowners or, in fact, of a traditional élite of natural rulers. The efforts of the educated élite are of course constrained by the state of the world economy; and again the élite itself is usually deficient in the skills necessary for business and industry. Nevertheless the élite is anxious to strengthen its power through the control of the national economy, either indirectly or directly through state corporations. Thus the élite is predisposed to favour growth of that economic system which has hitherto nourished it. In the states of Africa in particular, the western educated élite has, within the present generation, emerged from the traditional rural area. The efforts of the members of such an élite are directed not towards the redistribution of income in the society in such a manner as would alter their position relative to that of the humble farmers and craftsmen. They seek an expansion of the economy so that avenues of upward mobility for themselves might become more open and that privileged positions might be created for members of their families, local communities or castes. Hence the creation of new opportunities and moreover the over supply of applicants tends to exacerbate the expression of primordial sentiments as competition for power and for jobs is expressed in terms of ethnic, caste or religious categories.

The modern African state is, to a large extent, a meritocracy; its leaders have come from a wide variety of social strata and have reached high office by virtue of their superior education. But they are anxious that all their children should share the style of life into which they have been born and in which they have been raised. It would be an unusual parent who, having graduated from a university and earning between £1,000 and £3,000 a year, was happy at the prospect of his son terminating his education at the secondary level and earning but a fifth of his father's income. As it is, children of educated parents have great advantages in gaining entry to secondary school and universities, both in that they do better in competitive examinations and that their parents can afford the fees. The educated élite have a vested interest in maintaining an education system which is overtly egalitarian but yet favours them at the expense of lower strata.

There are few opportunities for the western educated élite to enter directly into significant entrepreneurial activity. Yet they do invest their savings in house property which, in the rapidly growing cities, can yield a lucrative return. Again, though civil servants may be debarred from private business they can establish close kin, and especially wives, in such enterprises and favour them with government contracts. The increased control over the economy through nationalization and state factories can give politicians and civil servants opportunities for graft; the commissions of inquiry recently held in Nigeria, for instance, show that they have not been slow in grasping these opportunities.

The African élite has been described as a 'class in formation'. Here as elsewhere in poorer nations, the two most vital questions are firstly, to what extent is the present élite able to perpetuate itself in the coming generations; how far will economic development permit the continuing recruitment from the less privileged homes? Secondly, how long will the masses tolerate the wide discrepancy in income between themselves and the élite? The answer to the second question will, in large measure, depend on the degree to which individuals feel that they or their children have a chance to share in the rewards of high office and power.

IDEOLOGIES AND POLITICAL PARTIES

In governing a state its élite has certain primary tasks; it must mobilize the masses in support of its rule. In the colonial territory, the indigenous élite must convince the colonial power of its popular support; the latter is apt to argue that its own provincially based officials can far more effectively represent the views of the rural peasantry than can western educated intellectuals, divorced from their traditional culture and ensconced in the affluent suburbs of the capital cities. The élite must therefore stimulate and support locally originating protest movements and formulate an ideology which defines their interest in and relationship with the masses. Once in power the élite becomes concerned to curb the local protest movements and the manifestation of its support is no longer the sporadic strike but victory through the ballot-box. Furthermore, as the ruling élite seeks to alter radically the structure of society, threatening scores of locally vested interests, so must its popular support be intensified. No longer is it enough for the masses to register a vote in support of the regime every few years; continually they must be prepared to try out innovations, make sacrifices, take risks.

The ruling élite must also promote consensus and reduce conflict within the state. Specifically it must foster unity among the sections of the élite with their varied interests. It must minimize tension between the privileged strata of society and the impoverished masses. In the following paragraphs we shall examine briefly two methods of attaining these ends – the development of ideologies and the establishment of political parties.

An ideology enshrines the popularly accepted ideas about the structure and processes of society, interpreting the society's history and providing a basis for the evaluation of new experience. It incorporates a statement of the goals and values approved by the society. In propagating an assuredly populist ideology the ruling élite can in fact be deceiving itself as to the degree of support which it enjoys among the masses – it can lull itself into a state of false confidence. Alternatively the ideology may be expressly used to manipulate the masses, to win acceptance of unpopular changes. Yet, as the leaders of many ex-colonial states have discovered, the degree of mobilization which was sufficient to bring them to power has proved quite inadequate in facilitating the revolutionary changes subsequently proposed.

The popular ideologies of the poorer nations are often embraced in the single term 'nationalism'. Yet this term covers too many discrete themes, not all of which may be dominant at any one period. Emphasis rests on national self-sufficiency and independence from the erstwhile colonial or imperial power. The cultural identity of the nascent nation is stressed. The western educated African or Asian, for instance, rebels in frustration against western culture and the western society to which he has sought entry as an equal; rather than be a second-class citizen of the West he returns to his own culture seeking to raise it so that it may stand equal to others in the modern world, rather than disparaging it as he had hitherto been inclined to do. By this process local variations in an indigenous culture tend to be oc-cluded. In the political sphere, nationalism stresses the right of the indigenous élites to manage the affairs of their own countries; and in more practical terms argues that the top positions in government be open to them. In the economic sphere national-ism embraces the complaints of the relatively poorly organized indigenous businessmen against the competition from the inter-nationally organized expatriate firms which tend to dominate the economy of their countries. The themes listed here obviously appeal primarily to the privileged sections of society; the masses are apt to argue cynically that the substitution of one set of rulers for another will not, of itself, change their fortunes. Hence, to win popular support the ruling élite must go beyond the themes of nationalism normally defined. (Conversely, of course, a party such as a communist party, which appeals speci-fically and directly to the urban workers or the rural peasantry, needs to stress these nationalist themes, in so far as it seeks the support of the privileged sections or at least tries to neutralize their opposition. Thus the Chinese Communist party in the 1920s relied heavily on a nationalist ideology.)

Gandhi

The name of Mahatma Gandhi will forever be associated with India's struggle for independence. Let us look therefore at his doctrines as an ideology representative of these common in the poorer nations: we must, too, see his teaching within the broad context of the independence movement.

The phases of Indian political activity have been admirably sketched by Desai.[9] From the mid nineteenth century a national consciousness began to develop among the western educated Indian intellectuals; but they sought to reform Indian society on western lines, introducing democratic rights such as a free press. These men founded the Indian National Congress. In the final decades of the century these men dominated the nationalist movement; they sought reform through constitutional means, believing that they could achieve their goals by appealing to the conscience of the British rulers. As unemployment grew among school-leavers so there developed a frustration with the policies of the liberal intellectuals, and extremist groups emerged which on one hand demanded full self-government and on the other placed greater stress on India's own cultural heritage. These extremists dominated the Congress in the first two decades of the twentieth century and in emphasizing Hindu culture alienated the Muslims who formed their own League; in their militancy they appealed to the 'lower middle classes'. In the later decades two parallel themes emerged. On the one hand there was an increased consciousness among the peasantry, the urban workers and outcastes who were subject to appeals from socialist and communist parties; but on the other hand, India witnessed the growing intensity of communal feelings. In some areas, religious divisions paralleled occupational ones – thus in Bengal the peasants were mostly Muslim, the landlords Hindu. In the urban areas, Muslims tended to be less well educated than Hindus and felt disadvantaged in the competition for jobs. Predominantly Muslim areas of India were the last to be penetrated by the British and were consequently less developed. Thus, although the Muslim League was itself dominated by a landed and business élite, within the Indian subcontinent economic rivalry was expressed in tension between religions. Desai argues that the privileged élite, either deliberately or by default, fostered this tension in order to detract from the growing consciousness of social class.

Gandhi was born in 1869, in a small princely Gujarat state lying on the Indian shores of the Arabian sea. He belonged to a Hindu high-ranking trading caste; both his grandfather and his father had served as prime ministers of the state. Situated at the meeting-place of Persian, Arabian and African influences in Indian culture, this part of Gujarat was noted for its intense religious eclecticism as several religious strains found expression in a variety of syncretic sects. Gandhi's own family was a devout one. He came to London to study law and seems initially to have tried to adopt the dress and manners of an English gentleman. Poverty and a change of philosophy later modified his goals though he nevertheless anglicized his family's clothing and the furnishings of his house on his return to India. Here his natural shyness and the consciousness of being ill at ease both in Indian and western society contributed to his failure to prosper in his profession. To escape, he sailed to South Africa where, subjected to discrimination as an Indian, he became so politically active that he quickly assumed a dominant role in Congress on his return to India in 1920.

Gandhi's success derives from the fact that 'through his way of life and specific reforms he advocated Gandhi could mitigate the ideological cross-currents of the urbanized élite. Indeed, he reflected every current of Indian sentiment and thought, but by not yielding to any he possessed a vantage point from which to appeal to all.'[10] Significantly, he died at the hands of a Hindu fanatic. His teaching is summarized in three concepts: Swaraj or political independence; Satyagraha or non-violent non-co-opera-tion; and Swadeshi or the revival of traditional village India. By these he appealed to the intellectuals, the landlords and business-men and to the peasant masses alike. In advocating social re-forms such as women's education, and in attacking untouch-ability and child marriage he attracted the western educated intellectual; yet these reforms were advocated within Hinduism and he could thus appeal equally to those who sought to uphold Indian traditions. He did not for instance attack the caste system as such, for he opposed intermarriage and commensality between castes. He favoured the protection of the cow while advocating model dairies!

In idealizing village life Gandhi appealed to the consciences of the urban élite whose rural origins were quickly being forgotten. He advocated rural development but in abjuring his followers to reject imported western tools and consumer goods and to return to the traditional loom he pleased not only the village craftsmen but also the Indian industrialists who sought a protected market. Again Gandhi did not attack property; for the peasant, the dig-nity of labour was stressed; for the landlord, the rewards of charity.

Gandhi's stress on non-violence was in many ways an effective weapon against British rule; for in that it demanded from his followers actions which could be legitimated by Hindu beliefs and which called for little personal risk, it was popular with the masses. But it also appealed to the intellectuals, and inasmuch as Gandhi opposed industrial strikes, to the business élite.

Gandhi's popularity did not of course rest upon his success in uniting the various sections of the Indian élite; it was as a holy man to whom they attributed extraordinary powers that the masses revered him – a man cast in a traditional Hindu role. Gandhi himself opposed such idolatry but in seeking to expiate the violence done in his name by further acts of self-denial he only enhanced his power among the masses who saw in his actions but a further manifestation of his holiness.

There were opponents to Gandhi during his lifetime but, in that they appealed to limited interests only, they were individually ineffective and never combined to form a rival movement. Since his death his teaching has fallen quickly into eclipse. The rapid increase in Indian military expenditure resulting from her wars with China and Pakistan as well as the need to maintain internal security, ill befit the philosophy of non-violence. The idealization of village life becomes equated with rural stagnation and is opposed especially by those who see rural development in terms of a radical alteration in social structure. Yet the Gandhian spirit lives on in such movements as the Bhodan which urges the landlords voluntarily to redistribute their land to the poor rather than wait for punitive legislation.

'Négritude' and African Socialism

If we move to West Africa for other examples, we find ideologies which have much in common with those of the Indian nationalist leaders. But here the majority of the members of the present élite were born in the rural area and have, therefore, much less inclination to become romantic about village life. Again, they belong to no great cultural tradition and face a rather different task in weaving from the variety of local but usually ill-documented cultures a heritage satisfying to themselves. In some West African states the emphasis placed on the ideology is much greater than in others. Intellectuals educated in France tend to be more philosophical, the English-trained men more pragmatic. Leaders such as Nkrumah who have sought to manipulate the masses are more in need of an ideology than those who practice *laissez-faire* policies. Two themes predominate in West Africa: *négritude* or the African personality, and African socialism.

Négritude has appealed especially to those who have been most completely assimilated to western culture – to the student from the French colonies fully accepted by his Parisian Left Bank peers rather than the Nigerian Ibo or Yoruba who lived in London virtually encapsulated in the society of members of his own ethnic group. For the former, the need is to provide for the system of values there acquired, a definite African content. This is sought in the tribal village – but not in the villages of any particular ethnic group but rather in an idealized community presumed to be universal in Africa. Thus *négritude* tries to transcend ethnic differences. The values stressed tend to be the antithesis of those which are believed to characterize western societies. Thus against the individualism and materialism assigned to the latter, *négritude* stresses the community and its values. Alienation, it is argued, is absent in traditional African societies – it is the epitome of western capitalist society. Such are the themes exhorted for instance by Senegal's philosopher-president Senghor, who studied and taught in France for many years, and who has a French wife. They seem to reflect the intellectual problems faced by the western educated élite in readapting to their own culture; the proponents of *négritude* do not consider whether the values extolled are appropriate to the rapid economic development which they also advocate.

The tribal village is furthermore described as a classless society, without conflict. Classes are seen as a phenomenon characteristic of western industrial society; but Africa need never experience them. The absence of conflict in tribal societies would not be accepted by social anthropologists; and they would certainly point to some African societies which were in the past quite rigidly stratified. Yet there are Africans today who will violently attack western scholars who describe their pre-colonial history in terms of conflict. Thus African leaders use the term socialist for their societies on the grounds that traditional

153

communities were so structured; by extension, modern African society is also socialist and classless.

The term socialist is also appropriate in that it describes the existing high degree of state control of the economy, a heritage of the colonial situation in which the metropolitan power built the railways, and provided almost all public services. It fosters the belief in planning and in the further extension of state control of trade and industry; this as we have already seen is readily acceptable to dominant educated élite in the higher civil service and public corporations.

South American Populism

In South America one does not find many comparable ideologies. Obviously the ruling élite of Spanish colonial, or even of recent European origin, will not seek its heritage in Indian cultures. Yet political leaders within this ruling élite must, to an ever-increasing degree, seek the support of the mass of the population – or at least of a significant section of it. But the popular appeals have in most cases been made to the urban workers; the peasantry has been ignored. Inasmuch as the appeals are made by the leaders of élitist parties and political groups the class interests of the workers are for obvious reasons not stressed; instead the ideologies stress a united people and a euphoria of nationalism directs hostility against an external enemy – usually the U.S.A. In this way the leaders can attract the support of a wide variety of groups which for one reason or another do not support the *status quo*; the appeal to the workers does not invalidate the appeal to sections of the élite experiencing relative deprivation. The success of the popular leader in attracting support depends, to a large extent, on the degree to which he can create a relationship of patronage with his followers; and this too inhibits the development of a class ideology. The main bases for support usually lie among the recent immigrants to the city, as yet unassimilated and unorganized.

The highly successful popular leader has the power to carry out reforms in his society. But popular movements of the type outlined above are usually opportunist, concerned mainly with securing short-term privileges for the leaders and their supporters; the heterogeneity of the interests represented vitiates long-term planning and results in ineffectual compromises.

Parties and Coalitions

The ideologies created by the intellectual élite have little appeal or relevance to the ill-educated urban and rural masses unless they are translated into simple slogans and are propagated by and in the name of a charismatic leader – a Gandhi or Nkrumah. They serve mainly to convince and assure the élite of its role in the developing society. Yet the masses must be mobilized at least to vote periodically and here the organized party is essential.

The party is founded and developed within élite groups. It tends to serve to transmit ideas and instructions to the masses rather than act as a vehicle for the expression of their interests. Inevitably the senior members of the party, the members of legislatures or the high-ranking organizers, are well-educated men; professionals tend to dominate. Take for example the membership of the Nigerian (Federal) House of Representatives in 1957: of the members elected from the Eastern and Western Regions over a third were university graduates, another third had complete secondary education and a further quarter had some post-primary education; these same men tended to be teachers (a quarter) or lawyers (a little over one fifth); almost a third were businessmen – the proportion from the Yoruba West being higher than from the dominantly Ibo Eastern Region. The representatives from the Northern Region were less well educated, though all but a sixth had received post-primary education; here two thirds of them were native authority and local government officials. Significant in most African states is the absence among the legislators of men who have risen to prominence through the trade-union movement; Sekou Touré of Guinea, the late Tom Mboya of Kenya and Kenneth Kaunda of Zambia are conspicuous exceptions. One might perhaps expect that the more radical parties have a leadership drawn from the less well-educated sections of the community; but this is usually not the case. Thus Segal writes,

It is astonishing, for instance, how many of India's senior communists, the proclaimed leaders in the struggle of the proletarian and peasant masses, speak and indeed think in English rather than the vernacular. One prominent communist organizer commented wryly: 'We read so many foreign books that we know more about the Italian Communist party than the French Communist party does!' And this hiatus between spokesmen and following is emphasised in the similarity of manner and method – a sort of cultural comradeship – between the leaders of Congress . . . and those of the Communist Party itself.[11]

As in other poorer nations, the educated Indian communist leadership seems more concerned with issues of dogma relevant to industrial societies than with the analysis of the problems of its own country in basic Marxist terms.

The élite-led party seeks popular support either by appealing to an undifferentiated public – an appeal to the masses in terms of nationalism, dignity, freedom and the like – or to specific interest groups, these being defined either in primordial or socio-economic terms. The same party might employ different approaches simultaneously. Thus the Action Group of Nigeria, in attempting to become a nationwide party in the 1959 Federal Election, used all three types of appeal. In the Western Region where it was already dominant it appealed to everyone, its slogan being 'Freedom for all, life more abundant'. In the non-Ibo areas of the Eastern Region and the non-Hausa areas of the Northern Region it exploited the fears of the ethnic minorities that they were being exploited and subjected by the dominant group. In the Hausa states it endeavoured to awaken, though with minimal success, the consciousness among the *talakawa* commoners of their conflict with the Fulani aristocracy.

One would expect a communist party to appeal specifically to the urban proletariat; but organized workers are few in number in the poorer nations and while they may certainly believe themselves to be exploited they also tend to be among the more secure and better-paid workers and therefore unlikely to engage in radical activities. So a communist party must appeal elsewhere. Here again, India provides a fascinating example. Harrison writes, 'Indian communism is a loose federation of regional units that have succeeded, where they have in fact succeeded, only on regional ground. The uneven pattern of communist strength corresponds to the pattern of identification with regional forces'.[12] Thus while the Indian Congress has been most firmly entrenched in the Hindu heartland, the communists have found most support in the non-Hindu south.

In part the pattern of Communist strength in India has coincided with those regions, such as Andhra and Kerala, where the sense of regional subjection in a multilingual political unit became most acute and where the Communist parties were able to outdo others in championing the demand for regional autonomy. . . . Only part of the answer, however, lies in the manipulation of regional patriotism. . . . It is where the Communist leadership at the same time holds a footing in politically strategic regional castes, which are in most cases rising non-Brahman castes, that Communist activities have gained decisive leverage. Indeed, divided as power is in every region among the new caste lobbies, regional caste ground is the only solid ground on which the manipulator can stand.[13] [In Andhra] the leadership exploit(ed) India's most intense regional agitation for autonomy; in addition Andhra leadership happened to be based in a politically strategic regional caste, the Kamma gentry of the Krishna-Godavari delta. With their base in the Kammas who own an estimated eighty per cent of the fertile delta land, the Andhra Communist leaders 'belonged' in their regional, and social and economic structure.[14] [The period of communist success came when the] Kammas had lost factional ground inside the Congress to the Reddis, a rival non-Brahman peasant proprietor caste group.[15] [Later, the Congress appealed to Kamma economic interests and regained some of their support.] Where regional Communist parties have been unsuccessful . . . it is because predominantly Brahman Communist leaderships have competed as social strangers for the allegiance of newly-assertive non-Brahman caste lobbies.[16]

Political leaders everywhere would like to win universal support, not least because they would wish to enjoy in perpetuity the pleasures and privileges of office. It is in the newly independent African states that single party regimes have, in so many cases, developed. Here the cultural and social differences within the élite have often been relatively slight and have, in addition been obscured by a pervasive ideology. The same ideology has stressed the classlessness of local society and hence the absence of conflicting groups on which a multi-party system could rest. Often the colonial power had actually stimulated the growth of rival parties arguing that a plurality of parties would render the independent state democratic. Yet we have seen the weaker parties decay, merge with their dominant rival or be legislated out of existence. Once in power the successful party can increase its strength inasmuch as the masses see it as the source of all social benefits. Vote for an opposition candidate and one may deprive one's constituency of the possibility of winning a new hospital or a tarred road; many constituencies have urged their member, elected on an opposition platform, to 'cross the carpet' and join the government party, The government controls most of the means of communication; and government information loudspeaker vans may not only be instructing the rural peasantry about the mechanics of voting but also reminding them for whom they should vote. Furthermore, the vernacular translation of the term 'opposition' may denote not 'alternative government' but 'wreckers and hooligans'.

The party seeking to mobilize the masses not only into electoral support but also to more positive action, will seek to control a wide variety of vital associations. Thus, in Nkrumah's Ghana, the trade unions, youth brigades, women's associations were all embraced within the Convention People's Party as constituent elements.

Why did not the western educated intellectuals, overtly subscribing to the ideals of 'democracy' and the like, protest against the development of single party regimes? Part of the answer lies in the fact that most were in government employ and that protest might have cost them their jobs. A move to overthrow the regime might also have endangered their privileged position in the state.

The single party is not of course necessarily unrepresentative of popular opinion – each member has been elected by his constituency. An important factor is the degree to which the party protects the privileged positions of its members by refusing to support alternative nominations at elections. In Eastern Nigeria in the mid 1960s the N.C.N.C. leadership sought to reward sitting members of the House of Assembly in giving them the party nomination; a number of men stood as 'Independent N.C.N.C.' candidates and won, they later were admitted into the N.C.N.C. In contrast, the party leadership in Kenya and Tanzania has, in recent elections, encouraged the proliferation of candidates, all loyal to the party, with the result that a considerable proportion of the more junior sitting members were replaced by newcomers; in contrast, most ministers retained their seats. The distinction emphasizes the importance of patronage in the single party system and the strains which occur as members of parliament become too securely ensconced in their seats.

With the passage of time members of parliament lose contact with their electorate; they become accustomed to the pleasures of life in the capital city and loyalties to their party begin to outweigh those to their constituencies. With relative economic stagnation they may be unable to fulfil the expectations of their people in providing social benefits for the community, jobs for individuals; they become reluctant to visit their constituencies empty-handed. The success of the ministers in Kenya and Tanzania seems to reflect their greater control over these benefits and hence their success as patrons. In *Man of the People*, Achebe draws a vivid picture of the local member of parliament – flattered by obsequious praises by those who had won favours and the many more who hoped to gain, until his sudden demise when both his enemies and his erstwhile followers revelled in his loss and demolished his reputation.[17] The fall of Nkrumah produced the same apparently sudden switch in public sympathy as even known C.P.P. supporters joined in the dancing in the streets. The single party system may result, though it does not do so in all cases, in a structure of highly personalized support and in the absence of a more institutionalized means for the expression of grievances. The incumbent local leader is rivalled by aspirants representing other factions which regard themselves as underprivileged; the success of the latter will in part depend on their success in manipulating primordial loyalties of ethnic groups or caste, or socio-economic interests.

In the monolithic party power resides mainly at the top, usually in the founding clique. But independence resulted not only in the need of the leadership to mobilize popular support but also in the devolution of power to regional legislatures and local government councils. These bodies are often more vital to the electorate as they may control the provision of local social services while the central legislature deals with the more remote themes of foreign affairs, defence and national communications. The strength of the party becomes increasingly dependent upon its control of these local and regional bodies and on the men who dominate them – men who are less likely to be the western educated intellectuals but are, rather, the local landowners and businessmen, traditional rulers, and a variety of other such opinion leaders. These men, too, are more likely to support local ethnic or caste lobbies perhaps even against national interest as conceived by the intellectuals.

The tendencies described in the previous paragraphs explain in part the decline of those dominant parties which seemed to have such universal support in the years immediately before and after the achievement of independence but which have since fallen apart. In 1970 the Indian Congress party was in a perilous position. For long it has contended with the opposition of social-ist and communist parties with their doctrinaire intellectual leadership but often regional and caste support. The Swatantra party representing in part business interests and the Jana Singh, the party of militant Hinduism, threatened it from the right. But how far are we correct in interpreting the tensions within the Congress in terms of personal rivalries and the left-right dichot-omy? This is certainly the explanation given by so many com-mentators. One important element was, probably, the Congress's local loss of support through a variety of shifts in caste and ethnic allegiances, changes which indirectly influence the strength of personalized factions at a higher level. Again, as we have already noted, the emergent local élites tend to be socially conservative and ethnically or caste oriented and out of sympathy with the intellectual party élite. Faced with a sudden loss of parliamentary support Mrs Gandhi, in a gesture towards popular feeling, nationalized the banks thus further alienating the business group in Congress and placing her at the mercy of the more extreme radicals in her own party and in socialist and communist parties. This support grew lukewarm when the Congress party failed to ensure the passage of legislation reducing the incomes of the princes and some of the privileges of the Indian Administrative Service. The privy purses of the princes were then abolished by Mrs Gandhi by a presidential decree; but this act was later de-clared by the courts to be unconstitutional. Ultimately the Con-gress party split. In the ensuing election campaign Mrs Gandhi travelled extensively and in a tightly-packed schedule of meetings appealed directly to the mass of the people. They rewarded her with a landslide victory in which she won two thirds of the parliamentary seats. None of the other parties – those of the extreme conservatives or radicals, or of the dissident Congress leaders – emerged with more than one fifteenth of the number of seats won by the Congress party. Mrs Gandhi's problems have turned from the search for tactical support in the lobbies of parliament to the satisfying of the economic and social aspirations of her new and vast electorate.

In some states the single party regime seems to have been a transitory phenomenon; in others it never developed. Instead perhaps we have a plurality of parties representing a number of different interests and loyalties. Government is possible only when some of these, together representing a majority of the electorate, form a coalition. We are apt to interpret this situation in terms of a European model, imagining that all parties lie on a spectrum from the conservative right to the radical left and that a coalition will be formed by adjacent parties. But as we have seen parties in the poorer nations are not so easily defined and some alliances seem to us rather strange. The clearest examples come from Latin American states where communist parties have supported military regimes with little or no overt invention of reform. But African examples are to be found. In the 1959 Federal Nigerian election the Action Group campaigned to win support as a national party; it had relatively little success and a coalition was formed between the Northern People's Congress, dominant in Northern Nigeria and representing the almost feudal Fulani aristocracy, and the N.C.N.C. of the Eastern Region representing some of the most westernized and achievement-oriented groups in the country. The Action Group which lay, socially, mid-way between these two, went into opposition. In their policies and general orientation the Action Group and N.C.N.C. were natural allies; yet ethnic rivalry divided the Yoruba and Ibo. The Northerners, for their part, were only too anxious to prevent a coalition against them.

The possibility of such alliances rests upon the fact that the dominant interests of the parties are not couched in socio-economic terms; a wide variety of interests are not therefore seen to be incompatible. The parties too are perhaps interested more in short-term benefits than in long-term change and horse-trading between the parties is carried on without either party seriously compromising its supporters. Again the minor parties in the coalitions expect that, in office, they will be able to develop their patronage and thus improve their chances at succeeding elections. (This must be balanced against the loss of prestige suffered, for example, by a communist party which associates with a conservative party.)

The parties of Latin America are, for such reasons, frequently described in the most cynical terms. They are unscrupulous in making election promises to the masses which remain unfulfilled. They are portrayed as instruments whereby factions within the élite manoeuvre themselves into power largely for their own gain. Even those parties such as the A.P.R.A. of Peru which came to power with a radical image and overwhelming popular support are, two decades later, concerned to maintain the social *status quo*.

In assessing the support received by political parties we must not neglect completely that given by external sources – specifically by the governments of the western powers; for in extreme cases they may virtually maintain an unpopular party in office. The methods used range from the direct – the contribution of money to party funds, the overt public support given to the party and its leaders, the military aid to reinforce its coercive powers; to the indirect – the provision of capital for development, which in increasing prosperity, enhances the popularity of the ruling party. But these are themes which merit a book in themselves.

8 Crises and Coups

The poorer nations of the world share a common characteristic – their economic dependence upon the industrial nations; and as they develop, so generally does this dependency increase; but so, too, does the income gap increase between poorer and industrial nations. The educated élite of the former have substantially assimilated the living styles shared by those men and women of similar occupation in the industrial states; and in consequence the cultural and material gap between them and the humble peasant or unskilled urban worker tends to grow ever wider.

REVOLUTIONARY CHANGE?

The previous chapters have, however, shown that further generalizations about the rate and direction of social change in the poorer nations are not easily made. We have discussed a number of variables. The traditional social structures differ widely from the fairly egalitarian tribal societies of Africa, to the peasant societies in which the farmer is dependent upon an almost feudal land-owning aristocracy and to the caste societies of India. Technological changes in the rural areas have not resulted in uniform change; as we saw from the examples of Wangala and Dalena in South India the introduction of modern irrigation and sugar-cane growing produced little structural change in the former village while the latter, exploiting newly available opportunities, experienced some quite radical changes. The clue to the different response seemed to be in the degree to which technological change resulted ultimately in alterations in the social rankings of individuals and groups within the community. In the rural areas, too, we saw that protests against the existing state of affairs might

163

range from millenarian movements, their adherents retreating to a world of fantasy, to the violent seizure and redistribution of land. In the rapidly growing urban areas we find, at one extreme, well-paid and secure workers employed in the technologically advanced factories, often foreign-owned enterprises; while such men may be well-organized into trades unions, their protests and demands may be muted by the fear of displacement by the unemployed. These latter, together with those who eke out a precarious existence in service occupations and the many who work only spasmodically, constitute the ever-expanding slum populations. Here the basic social units may not be the territorially defined ward but groups based upon common origin in village or caste. The life of the individual becomes encapsulated within those associations.

A further set of variables concerns the characteristics of the present educated élite. In the African states, this élite tends to have come, within the past generation, from homes spanning the entire social structure; some are sons of traditional chiefs but the parents of many were men who ranked relatively low in status in their communities. In a few African countries, and to a greater degree in India, we find third and fourth generations of educated families dominating the social scene. At the other extreme we have the Spanish colonial aristocracy of the South American states still monopolizing to a substantial degree the new opportunities provided by university education.

Each group in society makes demands relating to the distribution of power, prestige and wealth. For some, it is in their interest that the existing patterns should be preserved, thus maintaining their own ranking in society. Others demand either a redistribution of society's rewards to favour themselves, or seek improved channels of social mobility so that they can achieve existing rewards at the expense of their fellows. These demands are articulated with varying degrees of precision and vigour.

It is in the aggregation and resolution of these demands that societies change structurally. And such is the variety of possible patterns that we cannot postulate any dominant direction or rate of change. The outcomes are as varied as the demands. Stagnation is as likely as rapid social development: peaceful adaptation as likely as violent revolution. Nor may we equate peaceful adaptation with rapid change, revolution with stagnation; nor yet again revolution with rapid change.

Violence nevertheless does seem to be almost endemic in the poorer nations. Crudely one may assert that violence results whenever men feel that they have exhausted all the peaceful and institutionalized means of expressing their grievances – and in the poorer nations the institutionalized means are often weakly developed. But violent outbreaks take many forms. On the one hand we have the violence of the workers and peasants either towards specified ends – such as seizing land, or else quite un-structured – the urban mob violence. On the other hand we have the violent seizure of government by small groups of men. Thus in twenty states of Latin America there were fifty-six successful changes of government by extra-constitutional means in the thirty years 1935–64; twenty of these were in the five states – Venezuela, Colombia, Peru, Ecuador and Bolivia. Governments have been overthrown by force in sixteen of the newly indepen-dent states of Africa.

Violent changes of government broadly take two forms – the military coup and the revolution. In the former case, a military group seizes office from the political élite ostensibly to prevent further violence; it is apt to act near election time when a close result seems likely to result in fighting between followers of rival parties. Alternatively a civilian group may seize control of the state apparatus; this is a more rare occurrence, firstly because in most of the poorer nations opposition groups are not allowed to organize to the extent of posing a threat to the established rulers, and secondly because it assumes the collapse or defection of the existing military forces. (For as recent wars have shown, though a well-equipped army finds it extremely difficult to contain rural guerrillas, the latter are unable to defeat the former in open combat.) In applying the term revolution to the seizure of power by a civilian group, even though supported by an armed body of men, we imply that radical change of the social structure results. This is not inevitable; the fervour of the new rulers may become quickly dissipated and the long-term changes in the society may be minimal. Similarly, though the effect of the military coup is generally to maintain the *status quo*, or at least to prevent too radical a change in society, some military leaders have nevertheless effected such changes in society as to be described as 'revolutions from above'.

Peaceful adaptation and violent change are so often viewed as alternatives – the former to be desired, the latter deplored. Certainly the former will be favoured by those holding positions of power, wealth, or prestige in society for it gives them the greatest chance of maintaining these. Again the outcomes of violence are least predictable and therefore shunned by many. In sociological terms the dichotomy arises when we view society as a structure in a state of equilibrium. Essentially there is in this model a consensus as to the values of the society; conflict may exist but it is successfully mediated within the structure so that equilibrium is maintained. By some sociologists, society is defined as a system of tension management. Violence however marks a state of disequilibrium. The question is posed – what conditions lead to disequilibrium? Or how, in other words, do we predict violent changes in society? A number of antecedent factors have been postulated. Some argue that falling living standards create that greater discontent that leads to violence; others claim that revolutions have occurred in periods of material improvement. A more refined argument alleges that when a period of rising standards is halted by stagnation or decline, aspirations become suddenly frustrated, and violence results. But an examination of coups and revolutions in African and Latin American states seems to indicate that they occur in both the most and the least wealthy states and at times of relative affluence and of stagnation. In other words they are not determined by economic cycles.

Chalmers Johnson has set out three characteristics of the disequilibrated structure.[1] First, the ruling élite depends increasingly on the use of force to maintain its power; secondly, the ruling élite is unable to develop policies which maintain the support of these sections of the population usually supporting it; thirdly, the ruling élite is deprived of its chief weapon of enforcing social behaviour – the army. But valid though these conditions may be, they seem trite; for they do not tell us when any of these conditions will be fulfilled. One is simply stating that a ruling élite will be overthrown when it cannot cope with the demands made by various sections of the populace and when it has lost the authority and physical force upon which it depends.

How does a ruling élite cope with demands without jeopardizing its own position in society? Basically two courses are open to it. It may open further the channels of social mobility so that individuals from underprivileged groups may achieve positions of privilege and thus acquiesce in the overall stratification pattern. Or, it may concede a limited change in the patterns of distribution of privileges and rewards in favour of the underprivileged, yet without jeopardizing its own status. The actions of the ruling élite will depend too upon its perception of the situation, or more specifically upon the astuteness of its leading members. Every situation is, however, composed of such a complex set of variables that it must be studied independently. In general, one could assert that an intellectual élite employed in the public services and professions might be better able to accommodate demands than a landowning élite faced with demands from the peasantry for land redistribution; but the example of the Rajputs cited earlier illustrates how the more affluent section were far more successful in maintaining their position than were the poorer members.

Before concluding with some case histories of violence and rapid change in the poorer nations let us look briefly at the nature of the military coup.

MILITARY COUPS

Almost invariably the coup is carried out by officers of the armed services; it is therefore a coup by one section of the educated élite against another, for education has to an ever-increasing extent became a prerequisite for commissioned rank. (In contrast the rank and file are often drawn from the more backward parts of the country, for here alternative means of gaining wage employment are negligible.) But the officer corps does not always represent perfectly the composition of the élite as a whole. Reliable data are scarce but most writers believe that the officers in Latin American armies are being drawn increasingly from the middle strata of minor professionals, traders, teachers and the like, at the expense of the ruling oligarchies. In fact, the army is seen by these middle strata as one of the main channels of social mobility. In the African states the officers come from the same

167

varied backgrounds as the educated élite in general; but some ethnic groups have shown a preference for military service. Thus in Nigeria at the time of Independence, three quarters of the Nigerian officers were Ibo, one eighth were Yoruba and the remaining eighth came from the north, mostly from non-Hausa areas. The Ibo are not by tradition a militaristic people and the choice of the army as a career reflects more the limited employment prospects for secondary-school-leavers in the late 1950s.

Soldiers are generally well paid. In African states, privates earn as much as skilled urban workers and N.C.O.s receive the equivalent salary of non-graduate teachers or highly-skilled artisans. Officers salaries are similar to those of university graduates with a Nigerian second lieutenant for instance starting at £768 a year and a brigadier at £2,700. The officers thus enjoy a style of life similar to other members of the educated élite. Yet much of this life is within the barracks and far from public gaze. African army officers tend to be relatively young, due to their recent rapid promotion as a result of Africanization. In Latin America, where armies have been locally officered for many decades, many senior officers have been prematurely retired to make way for more highly-trained juniors; subsequently these retired men in civilian life provide a vital link between the armed services and the community.

The armies of the poorer nations tend to be small. The independent African states were heirs to colonial forces largely designed to maintain internal security. Thus Nigeria with a population of over 50 million had an army of but 10,000. Ghana in 1967 had an army of 14,000 for a population of 8 million. Latin American armies tended to be larger – thus Peru, 45,000 for a population of 12 million, and Colombia 23,000 for 19 million. The armed services are highly professional organizations. Much of their equipment comes from abroad and a high proportion of the officers have received their training in overseas military academies where they tend to assimilate the values prevailing in these institutions. It is alleged that the traditions of Sandhurst are retained with more vigour in the Indian Army than in the British. In the British tradition, the training received by officer cadets is largely military in character. In contrast the instruction given at the Centro de Altos Estudos Militares in Peru includes the theory and practice of administration and economic planning; some of the teaching is by civilians and reaches very high academic standard. Many of the reforms carried out in this country in the 1960s had been worked out by the military experts in the C.A.E.M. Again, though the armies are small they absorb a large share of the national budget – often between 10 per cent and 20 per cent in Latin American states. The armed services are thus well trained and disciplined forces with a strong sense of their identity and cohesion.

An important variable is the view held by the military élite of their role in the state. On the one hand, the army may see itself as a professional body, under ultimate civilian command; on the other hand it may be a political army, considering itself responsible for the definition and delegation of political authority. Latin American armies in the states discussed here are all of the latter type; African armies fell into the former category, though the experience of political power will surely alter their conceptions of their role.

Perhaps the aspect of the military coup so frightening to the political élite is the ease with which it is carried out. Within a few hours, often bloodless, a small military force arrests the erstwhile leaders, takes over the hubs of communication and transport, and patrolling the streets ensures that popular feeling remains muted. Success is achieved with but a few men simply armed and with ordinary transport, often in spite of glaring incompetence and bungling by the participants. In Latin American states the coup is an endemic phenomenon, in tropical Africa the first successful coups – in Congo-Kinshasa, Togo and Dahomey – undoubtedly provided inspiration for neighbouring countries.

The timing of the coups seems to depend on a number of factors; for example imminent widespread violence occasioned by strikes or mob rioting which the political leaders seem unable to control is one clue to military take-over. In several Latin American states, as in Sierra Leone, the coup has followed a hard and close-fought election which either gave rise to doubts as to the real victor or suggested that a popular party had triumphed over that of the existing élite. The absence from the capital of the supreme political leader, who was thus unable to rally support to foil the army's bid for power, gave the military leaders of Ghana and Mali, for example, an opportune moment to act.

The popular reaction to military coups is generally one of mass support. The army leaders justify their extra-constitutional action in claiming that they have acted to preserve the integrity of the state. In Latin America many of the national heroes of the nineteenth century were military men and the army consequently has high prestige. In Africa a greater emphasis is placed upon elimination of corruption in public life. The army, so recently under expatriate leadership was seen as being largely above suspicion in contrast to other spheres; in Nigeria for instance, disillusion with the educated élite increased as it was discovered that not only were the political leaders often highly venal, a fact already well known, but that many senior civil servants and university professors too were using their offices for considerable private gain. The mass support for the coup comes from the thousands who have criticized patronage largely because it has brought little reward for themselves. But the stability which is promised by a military regime has obvious attraction for men of property too.

The army cannot be seen however simply as an arbiter between rival political groups. It has well-defined interests of its own, and is liable to act to preserve these when they are threatened. Thus the younger and more highly trained officers of the Bolivian Army revolted in 1932 after the generals, drawn from the oligarchy had failed so disastrously in the war against Paraguay. Some of the political leaders of the newly independent African states have from the outset been nervous of the ex-colonial army in the wings; Nyerere for instance tended to ignore the army, believing that Tanzania could be built without it. Other leaders have tried to create a small specialized force under direct control of the president and party, thus derogating from the power and prestige of the army. The threatened creation of such a force probably sparked off the coup in Mali which deposed President Keita, and it undoubtedly figured in the hostility of the Ghanaian army towards Nkrumah. The military leaders who have assumed power in Africa have done so with much overt reluctance and modesty. They have quickly incorporated civilian advisers into their governments and promised speedy

return to civilian rule – promises which have already been fulfilled in Sierra Leone and Ghana. In Latin America, in contrast,
the dividing line between generals and politicians becomes increasingly hard to draw as the former clearly hold political ambi-
tions and it is merely a tactical issue whether they govern directly
or through an apparently elected popular leader.

So far we have stressed the social cohesion existing within the
military services. In fact the same latent divisions tend to exist
within the army as within the national élite as a whole. Competition may exist between branches of the services and the police
over the allocation of defence expenditure and their respective
role in the state. In Tanzania, Kenya and Uganda, army mutinies occurred in 1964 largely over conditions of pay and prospects for promotion among the lower ranks. These divisions
were manipulated by politicians and, in the case of Tanzania, the
mutiny nearly led to the collapse of the government. Here, as in
the other two states, the political leaders called for British troops
to restore their control of the army. A consequence of the Tanzanian mutiny was the disbanding of rebel contingents and the
building of a new military force through the machinery of
T.A.N.U. the dominant political party. Furthermore as armies
have become rapidly modernized a generation gap emerges
between the senior officers and their more highly-trained juniors;
in Latin America this may be correlated with differences in social
origin – oligarchy versus the middle strata; in Africa the division
lies between the most senior officers, often promoted from the
non-commissioned ranks where as primary-school-leavers they
began their service as clerks and storekeepers, and the more
recently commissioned products of secondary school and university. Finally, though the camaraderie of barrack-room and
military academy may substantially occlude ethnic differences
within the armed services, when these divisions predominate in
the society at large, so will they threaten the army. The tragic
events in Nigeria amply illustrate this point. Again the succession
of coups in Sierra Leone arose in part from rivalry between the
creoles of Freetown and the Mende of the interior.

What may we generalize about the outcome of the military
coup? In the first place it curbs normal political activity, parliaments are dissolved and parties may be banned. But military rule

does not necessarily mean that popular opinion is less freely expressed; censorship regulations may in fact be relaxed. A military regime is however autocratic – and in the African states resembles strongly the pattern of colonial rule. The military leaders may rely heavily upon civilian administrators for advice and support. In African states, senior civil servants often argue that policies outlined by them are judged by the army leaders more rationally and with less prevarication than by the erstwhile politicians. But while a military regime may, by its administrative efficiency, implement reforms which the politicians have discussed and subsequently shelved, it seems in most cases far less able to conceive new solutions to the urgent problems of the poorer nations – the growing urban unemployment for instance.

At one extreme a military coup, may, in fact, restore power to a conservative oligarchy whose politicians have lost popular support. At the other, military leaders may carry out reforms which the politicians have been unable or unwilling to implement. But military leaders are usually hostile towards the demands made by the masses and their popular leaders. The civilian regimes which follow military rule are, in most cases, less radical than those which preceded it. A striking exception here is provided by Sierra Leone where military rulers handed over power to Siaka Stevens, a politician with strong trade-union backing who had, in fact, been victorious in the earlier election; but the military in this case were non-commissioned officers who had just ousted their senior officers.

SOME CASE STUDIES

Nigeria

Many of Nigeria's problems derive ultimately from the fact that three large ethnic groups – the 15 million Hausa, the $9\frac{1}{2}$ million Ibo and the 9 million Yoruba – constitute two thirds of the nation's population. Each group furthermore has dominated one of the three major administrative units into which Nigeria has been divided since the beginning of the colonial period. Cultural differences between neighbouring ethnic groups in West Africa tend to be great. Thus between the Yoruba and Ibo the difference is, very crudely, of the same order as between the English and the Russians. Greater differences separate these two peoples and the predominantly Muslim Hausa. Within each group, consciousness of a separate cultural identity has been increased in recent decades – by the jihad at the beginning of the nineteenth century, when a Fulani aristocracy seized power in most of the Hausa states and, among the Yoruba and Ibo, by a cultural renaissance among the western educated élite. Furthermore, cultural differences between these three groups are paralleled by equally marked structural variations. The Hausa–Fulani emirates are, in scale and political complexity, equal to the kingdoms of medieval Europe; the Ibo in contrast, live, as already described, in small village groups. The Muslim Hausa always regarded the pagan southern peoples with disdain. However western influences penetrated the south well before the north and while first the Yoruba and somewhat later the Ibo avidly accepted education, the British Colonial government, in an effort to uphold the Islamic faith and consequently the political structure of the emirates, banned mission activity in the emirates. As a result the southern regions of Nigeria were able in the mid 1950s to institute universal primary education while in Sokoto province, the Fulani heartland, less than 5 per cent of the children were attending school.

Economic competition between individuals and the contest for power in the new nation have both followed the ethnic divisions. With so few educated Hausa, it was the literate Ibo, unable to find employment in their home area, who moved into the northern towns as clerks and artisans. Retaining a strong loyalty to the places of their birth they tended to monopolize these occupations, placing their kin in vacant posts. In the 1960s the Hausa began to resent increasingly this exclusion as they produced literate youths qualified for these jobs. In the arena of federal government in Lagos the Yoruba and Ibo competed for posts of high power, wealth and prestige and, as the output of secondary schools and universities increased, competed for employment of any type commensurate with their education. Failure to achieve one's expectations was interpreted in terms of ethnic favouritism. Thus these two ethnic groups struggled to control the civil service, public corporations and even the University of Ibadan (where the Ibo Vice-Chancellor was challenged in the courts by the Yoruba Registrar, who alleged wrongful dismissal and mis-management of university funds). The Hausa, politically domi-nant, resented their inability to provide well-educated candi-dates for these posts and frequently tried to install in them men of lower qualifications, thus overtly replacing ascribed status in the Fulani aristocracy for education as the legitimate criterion for social mobility.

The struggle for political control of the Federal government was intensified by the fact that the Fulani aristocracy feared that, should a coalition of Ibo and Yoruba be dominant, their entire social structure would be threatened. Thus the Northern People's Congress, the party of the Fulani, in 1953 largely opposed the Yoruba Action Group and Ibo N.C.N.C. in their call for rapid moves towards self-government. Rioting resulted in Kano between Hausa and southerners. But realizing the in-evitability of independence, the N.P.C. strove to dominate the Federation. In the Federal parliament the Northern Region had more seats than Eastern and Western Regions together, the dis-tribution being based upon the 1952 Census. The reality of northern domination became apparent only when in the late 1950s each party became overwhelmingly dominant in its own region. The leaked results of its 1961 Census appeared to end this numerical superiority and after much political manoeuvring a new census was taken which substantially restored the *status quo*. Co-operation between Yoruba and Ibo in challenging the validity of the census was, as on so many other issues, vitiated by the competition between them. The N.P.C. formed an alliance with the N.C.N.C. after the 1959 Federal election, leaving the Action Group in opposition. Ideologically N.P.C. and N.C.N.C. were the furthest removed from each other; but the latter party was encouraged to accept the junior political role by the opportunity it received to dominate the administrative structure.

The origins of the military coup of January 1966 lie in the breakdown of law and order in Western Nigeria. In 1959 the Action Group, led by Chief Obafemi Awolowo, had campaigned, though not too successfully, throughout Nigeria, appealing for instance to the non-Ibo of the Eastern Region as an ethnic min-ority and to the commoners of the emirates as an oppressed class. The campaign did however threaten the dominance of the Fulani aristocracy. But it also led to the split within the Action Group, Chief S. L. Akintola leading the faction which preferred to keep the Action Group as a regional party. Ideological differences were paralleled by intra-Yoruba ethnic differences. A fracas in the Ibadan parliament led to the imposition of Federal administrative rule and the exile of leading politicians. But while Awolowo was ultimately gaoled for treason, Akintola was restored as regional premier and thus seen as an ally of the N.P.C. He was unpopular in many parts of the region and the first election in 1965 which would have validated his claim to authority was widely believed to have been rigged. The campaign was marked not only by an appeal for Yoruba unity through anti-Ibo slogans but also by much violence between rival political groups. This violence continued after the election and highway robbery on the road from Ibadan to Lagos made travelling very dangerous – especially to the élite.

The coup of January 1966 was staged by a group of middle-ranking army officers, who abducted and killed the Federal Prime Minister, Sir Abubakr Tafawa Balewa, and his minister of finance, and assassinated in their homes the premiers of the Western and Northern Regions, together with their wives. The officers were politically radical – Major Nzeogwu set up a Revolutionary Council in Kaduna, the capital of the Northern Region. They were also all Ibo, though this was probably of minor significance; most officers of this rank were Ibo and the conspirators would reasonably have excluded members of other ethnic groups from their plans. The occasion for the coup seems to have been the belief that Chief Akintola had asked the N.P.C. leaders for the support of the Nigerian Army in quelling the disturbances in the Western Region.

The coup seems to have misfired in Lagos and control passed to the supreme army commander General Ironsi – himself an Ibo. In Kaduna Major Nzeogwu handed over to Colonel Hassan, a son of the emir of Katsina. Military rule was widely welcomed throughout the country. But it took on an increasingly Ibo flavour. It was pointed out that only one Ibo officer had died in the coup, compared with four northerners and two Yoruba, and that though the Ibo political leaders of Eastern and Mid-Western Regions fled from their capitals, their lives were never endangered. Ironsi seemed to be surrounded largely by Ibo advisers. The officers promoted to fill the vacancies caused in the coup were almost entirely Ibo. Most important of all however, the military leaders, abetted by the senior civil servants, produced a plan to unify the administration of the country hoping thereby that the dominance of one region and its political party, the N.P.C., would be ended. But not only were the architects of this plan Ibo, but the scheme was seen to provide the Ibo with an opportunity to dominate the Federation through their educational achievements and aggressive clannishness. Rioting broke out in northern towns in which Hausa mobs killed many Ibo; the exodus of Ibo to the region of their birth began.

In July 1966 northern troops massacred a number of Ibo officers and other ranks in their barracks, together with General Ironsi, who was visiting Ibadan, and his host, the Western Region military governor. Colonel Gowon eventually assumed the supreme command of the army as the only senior officer acceptable to all factions – he was a Christian from a small 'pagan' ethnic group in the north. This appointment, however, increased dissension among the officers, for Gowon was junior to some of the regional military governors, notably to Ojukwu. In August and September renewed massacres of Ibo in the north intensified the exodus of refugees until almost none were left; thousands too left Lagos and Ibadan, especially among the educated élite though their lives were in little real danger; many semi-skilled workers justifiably feared unemployment at home.

Ibo plans for secession from the Federation began at least with the July coup and well before the subsequent massacres. The educated élite determined to form its own state, or perhaps a largely autonomous unit within a loose confederation, rather than endure Yoruba competition within a country still dominated by northerners. From similar motives the Yoruba vacillated – until the appointment of Chief Awolowo, earlier released from goal, as the senior civilian member of the federal government. Protracted negotiations led ultimately to the secession of the Eastern Region as Biafra and the commencement of a 'police action' by Federal forces to restore the integrity of the state.

The Biafran secession was complicated by the fact that most of Nigeria's oil lay within its territory; in offering oil rights to

French companies Colonel Ojukwu not only stimulated international rivalry but ensured a supply of arms. The Catholic missions, the dominant Christian body in Biafra, fostered overseas support and organized the supply of both munitions and relief. But the oil-wells lay mostly in non-Ibo areas and though many non-Ibo would have initially supported the Biafran secession, their obvious exclusion from governing councils and the atrocities perpetrated by Ibo soldiery as they were pushed back into the Ibo heartland, quickly alienated them. Notwithstanding the radical ideology of some of the officers who staged the January coup and the existence of radical pressure groups within Biafra, the new state showed few signs of an original ideological orientation. Though the world was continuously presented with descriptions of starving Ibo children, the educated élite within Biafra seem to have lacked neither food nor petrol for their cars. Cohesion was maintained despite the continual allegations, invariably repudiated by international observers, of genocide. With the collapse of Biafra the educated Ibo were quick to return to Lagos to attempt to reoccupy their former offices.

The effect of nearly three years of civil war was undoubtedly damaging to Nigeria's economy. Funds which might have been used for economic development maintained the army, now grown to 200,000 men. (Recruitment has been a partial solution to urban unemployment; fears grow that demobilization will lead to urban violence.) Import controls and restrictions on the export of money have cramped ostentation among the élite. But the social structure of the south seems to have been little affected. Politically, the major change has been the creation of three states from the former Eastern Region, the Ibo being in one of them, and six states from the Northern Region. In the consequent federation of twelve states, Hausa–Fulani domination will be virtually impossible. Within the north, military rule has effected some highly significant changes. For instance in withdrawing local courts from the direct control of the emirs, the power of the latter has been weakened. In fact the creation of more states may have been welcomed by the Fulani aristocracy in that it would enable them to maintain, within their traditional kingdoms, powers which in a regional structure would be surrendered to bureaucrats – and non-Hausa northerners at that.

Colombia

'No other country of Latin America – and few nations of the world – have in the mid twentieth century experienced internal violence and guerrilla war as has Colombia. The struggle in the Cuban mountains prior to Fidel Castro's ascent to power on 1 January 1959 pales in extent, if not in its consequence, tempered to the virtual civil war which ravaged the Colombian countryside in the years after 1948. The number of combatants is difficult to estimate, but between twenty and thirty thousand at the peak of violence may not be too high a figure.'[2] It is estimated that between 100,000 and 200,000 people lost their lives in '*la violencia*' between 1948 and 1964.

Civil war had been endemic in Colombia in the nineteenth century, but with the exception of localized outbreaks at election times, the first half of the twentieth century was one of comparative peace and stability with continuous civilian government. Political power was exercised by an élite which was socially undifferentiated but split into rival factions between which government alternated.

Though sharing most of the characteristics of the oligarchies of Latin American states, the Colombian élite has been rather more open than some others – that of Peru, for instance. A relatively high proportion of Colombian industry is indigenously owned, and the major expatriate investment is in oil – though the proportion invested in manufacturing industry is increasing. Although much of this commercial activity is controlled by families of the traditional aristocracy, there has been a considerable mobility into the Colombian élite of small businessmen from lower strata. And while the possession of landed estates remains the hallmark of élite status, the economic interests of the élite are diverse. As Dix remarks, 'Its values and goals have to an important extent become modernizing ones and the sources of élite power have become more pluralistic.'[3]

The 'middle class', though growing numerically so that it is now said to number 15 per cent of the total population, is still lacking self-awareness. Many in this stratum have fallen from élite status – and hope to regain it. Prosperous peasants in the rural area have few links with clerks and teachers in towns. The urban workers, as elsewhere, are mostly recent migrants, and are divided sharply between those with regular and well-paid jobs and the spasmodically underemployed and unemployed. High aspirations breed frustration, but Colombia's urban poor are far less centralized in one capital city than is the case in other states; they are poorly organized.

Colombia has few pure Indians – three quarters of the population is *mestizo* and almost all the remainder are white. Coffee, which provides between two thirds and four fifths of the country's foreign exchange, is produced mainly by independent small farmers; but these form but a small minority of the country's rural population. A third of farm properties are uneconomic *minifundia*; nevertheless the *hacienda* dominates the pattern of land distribution. Agricultural development has been marked in Colombia in recent decades.

Although a brewery was opened in the 1890s, industrial development in Colombia did not get under way until the 1920s. The following decades showed an increasing divergence in the ideologies of the two major parties, though the leadership remained identified with rival élite factions, and much of the following was secured by ties of patronage. The Conservatives represent order and hierarchy; the Liberals espouse the doctrines of nineteenth-century western liberalism, stressing liberty and popular rule. The urban masses have tended in recent years to vote Liberal rather than Conservative. Nevertheless economic interests still do not closely parallel party alignment – many merchants are Conservatives and many landowners are still Liberal supporters.

In 1934 President Lopez, a Liberal, came to power in a free election and inaugurated a programme of reforms influenced perhaps by the A.P.R.A. in Peru, by the New Deal in the United States, as well as by local socialist intellectuals. These reforms were largely directed by the modernizing segments of the Colombian élite, though supported by the urban workers and middle strata. Measures included an increased state control of economic development, a labour code, a mild land reform, improved education and health facilities. Yet the full effect of these was lost through the government's inability to control the local level administration, even its own party officials. Lopez's regime strengthened indigenous business interests which eventually turned against him, demanding economic *laissez-faire* policies rather than increasing control by intellectuals; it antagonized the entrenched élite without obtaining vital and active support from urban workers or middle strata. Lopez was followed by an essentially conservative ruler, though he later regained the presidency which he held until 1946.

'The Liberals had fostered the organised articulation of popular demands, and encouraged the expectation of their satisfaction, without having the will or the political strength to confront fully the implications.'4 The party became divided, the leadership of the radical segment being assumed by Jorge Eliécer Gaitan. Gaitan was a lawyer with a university education but he came from a humble home and had risen to prominence through the Liberal party hierarchy, briefly holding office as mayor of Bogota. His ideology seems inconsistent, incorporating strands of Italian fascism, Peruvian Aprista doctrines and old-fashioned liberalism; he argued not for radical structural change or the wholesale redistribution of wealth but for reforms – improved health and educational facilities, nationalization of public services, tax and electoral reforms. What differentiated Gaitan from other leaders was his direct appeal to the masses and his specific denunciation of the Colombian élite. Gaitan contested the presidential election in 1946 but came third, though obtaining nearly half of the Liberal vote in spite of the fact that he lacked official party backing. Soon he became virtual leader of the Liberal party though it refused to implement his policies. In a period of tension, Gaitan was assassinated in April 1948 – by a man who probably had a personal grievance against him. Spontaneous mob violence erupted in the streets of Bogota. Left-wing political groups tried to direct these towards the overthrow of the government but their own lack of organization and the traditionalist ties of the urban masses to the Liberal party vitiated these attempts. A more conservative government came to power in the capital and *la violencia* dominated the rural areas.

Before detailing the nature of this peasant rebellion, let us complete the chronicle of Colombian government. The repressive Conservative rule of President Gomez failed to bring peace to the countryside and in 1953 the army commander General

Rojas assumed power amid popular rejoicing. The small Colombian army had hitherto played a relatively inactive role in politics, especially since its own revolt had misfired in 1944. But, recently strengthened by U.S. aid and training and with the breakdown of law and order, it fulfilled its usual Latin American role. With a majority of civilians, most of them Conservatives, in his cabinets, Rojas was pledged to purify the party so as to fit it for national rather than sectarian leadership. He tried to end rural violence by giving an amnesty to prisoners, and many guerrillas disbanded; his government undertook a number of social welfare projects. But Rojas's regime became increasingly dictatorial and he alienated the support of the oligarchy and the church. He attempted to build himself into a populist leader appealing to the workers in the manner of Argentine's President Peron; but in spite of his increasingly anti-oligarchic proclamations he did little to change the country's social structure. In 1957 he was forced out of power by the concerted efforts of the oligarchy and a national front was established in which the Liberals and Conservatives were alternately to hold the presidency, 'in order', as President Lleras put it, 'that the national governing class might dedicate itself for sixteen years to realizing a gigantic effort of progress and justice, without tearing itself to pieces'.[5] Rojas contested the presidential election in 1962 but won only 2 per cent of the votes. In 1970, however, in a fair and closely contested election he won almost half of the votes against a Conservative National Front candidate. In advance of the final results of the count he declared himself the victor and mobs of his supporters surged through Bogota.

'*La violencia*' arose out of the superimposition of Colombia's crisis of modernization on the patterns of the country's hereditary hatreds.[6] At first the fighting was largely between Conservative and Liberal supporters, each apparently believing that the political dominance of the other would jeopardize their own property, honour and life. Local bureaucrats victimized their people, who in turn formed groups for self-defence. But economic motives soon became important. Farms which were abandoned were seized by the aggressors; in some areas gunmen were hired to terrorize farmers so that they fled or sold their land at a minimal price, often leaving a harvest ready for the assailants.

Some allege that the middle peasants used such activities to gain wealth and power in a quasi-feudal society which denied them other opportunities. Few areas of Colombia escaped *la violencia*; but it seems to have been least pronounced in areas dominated by large traditionally organized estates; it does not seem to have been correlated with low levels of education and lack of property. In fact it reached its height in areas where cash cropping brought higher incomes and where there was recent settlement of migrants; in other words violence was resorted to by those involved in changes which had already undermined the traditional social structure.

The guerrilla bands lacked both centralized command and a uniform ideology. Most were led by Liberal supporters though the party caucus disowned them; only a small minority were communist led. Most bands were of spontaneous local development with specific objectives – attacks on local officials, seizure of land. Very infrequently were class goals stressed. In this situation ties with urban workers who might have provided allies in the struggle were not sought. Nevertheless some guerrilla bands were of considerable size and contained a hierarchy of units with officers bearing military titles; members wore uniforms, sang guerrilla hymns and often lived according to stringent rules. Their activities were sometimes extremely savage, whole families being massacred and the bodies dismembered, as if the cohesion of the guerrilla band depended upon the common violation of the generally accepted norms of the society.

The advent to power of General Rojas considerably reduced the violence; and when Conservatives and Liberals formed the National Front, guerrilla activities began to wane. Serious attempts were made to rehabilitate the guerrillas and meet some of their demands. Furthermore, the Colombian army had now been trained in anti-guerrilla warfare and was at last able to mount successful operations. In the 1960s the bands which continued to function were those with a more extreme radical and ideologically oriented leadership. Rural violence was paralleled by urban terrorism with bombings and kidnapping in Bogota and other cities.

Even though it was anarchy rather than revolution (as some of its supporters claimed) *la violencia* has left its mark upon the countryside. Its leaders were usually peasants and not urban intellectuals and the peasantry is increasingly conscious of its own strength and interests. Demands for social justice and social services increased. Guerrilla activity destroyed many traditional norms and institutions, even if it permanently replaced them by nothing new; it created new roles in society and emphasized team work. The incursion of the army into the countryside brought to these areas a greater awareness of urban life and norms.

For a short period violence benefits the ruling élite by dividing the peasantry; but in starting new social processes it begins to change the structure of society and it is tempting to see, in the votes won by General Rojas, the increased consciousness of the peasantry.

Peru

In October 1968 General Velasco Alvarado took over the government of Peru from President Belaunde in a military coup which seemed typical of Latin American states. In the following June he announced, and his government is clearly intending to implement, a programme of land reform more radical than any that has taken place in the continent save only Cuba. Furthermore these reforms were promoted in the absence of any great pressure from the peasants themselves – the peak of their rebellion had markedly subsided since 1963 in face of considerable repression.

Peruvian political life has for many decades been dominated by an oligarchy of 'forty' families. Many of these do not derive from the colonial aristocracy but from recent immigrants who made their initial wealth in business. But the *nouveaux riches* acquired landed estates and the oligarchy is, in fact, still associated more with landowning than with individual entrepreneurship; nevertheless the oligarchy are prominent in banking and in expatriate dominated enterprises. They constitute a network of families controlling the wealth of the country. In consequence Peru had remained one of the more conservative of South American states.

Another feature of Peruvian society is the marked dichotomy between the creoles on the one hand, living in the capital Lima and on the coastal plain, working in plantations and mines, and the Indians on the other hand, outnumbering the former group by two to one, who live in the high Sierra in backward villages and latifundia.

From 1872–1919 the oligarchy ruled through military leaders even though the latter were often of modest social origin and had mixed blood. Political activity revolved around competition between rival factions within the oligarchy. The military was expected not to concern itself with commercial and monetary policies. The 'middle class' was poorly developed in the relative absence of bureaucratic cadres and independent entrepreneurs; it tended not to evolve its own value system or to have a distinct political ideology; rather was it dependent upon the oligarchy. The Indians had no voice in the government at all.

In 1923, Haya de la Torre, an exiled intellectual founded the Alianze Popular Revolucionaria Americana (A.P.R.A.), a party which has been described as populist. Torre himself was, and still is, a spell-binding orator; his party developed an intricate and powerful grass-roots organization. His policies were proclaimed as revolutionary and included the ending of dependence upon foreign powers, the improvement of the lot of the urban workers through trade-union activity and the organization of the peasantry. It explicitly appealed to the Indians. A coalition of middle strata, workers and Indians would have posed a serious threat to the ruling oligarchy. But the Apristas never managed to create this coalition – the Indians were too traditionalist to be impressed by its ideology, the mass of the workers lacked organization. The party's main strength lay, in fact, in the organized workers of the coastal plantations and factories and the poorer members of the middle strata. An avowedly Marxist party, which made stronger endeavours to win Indian support, correspondingly lost the vote of the urban workers.

Torre lost the election in 1931, and for sixteen months led an open insurrection against the government. He won in 1936 but the elections were cancelled by military rulers, though repression of his party was reduced. By 1950 the A.P.R.A. had lost much of its revolutionary zeal, becoming more accommodating towards the oligarchy. Splits developed in the party between the reformists seeking power and the outright revolutionists.

Nevertheless the oligarchy, under the name of one party or another and with military assistance, remained in power until 1962 when the first fully democratic elections were held. Of the three candidates General Odira, a former President, had no interest in land reform. Belaunde Terry, an architect, advocated a basic structural change in society; he appealed specifically to Indians and promised them land reforms; a capitalist economy was however to be retained on the coast. These policies differed but little from those of Torre, the third candidate. When it seemed likely that the A.P.R.A. had won the election, the military declared it fraudulent, took over power and arranged fresh elections in the following year. This time a coalition led by Belaunde won most votes, though a minority of the total. Torre joined Odira who had once exiled him and tried to suppress the Apristas by force, to form an opposition; the two groups substantially sabotaged the reforms introduced by Belaunde – even though these had long been advocated by the A.P.R.A. The Apristas understandably lost prestige among the masses.

Political movements of the extreme left did not grow powerful in Peru. Disgruntled members of A.P.R.A. and students formed a number of communist parties and members of some of these formed guerrilla bands in the rural mountain areas. In a few areas the peasantry was successfully encouraged to seize land but generally the bands failed to win the support of the Indians – they were usually composed of educated creoles who could not speak the Indian language. In 1965 General Velasco organized a nationwide anti-guerrilla campaign which resulted in the capture of most of the leaders; the latter were not tried however and remained relatively free to proselytize until 1969.

General Velasco's coup ended a period of weak and ineffective government. Belaunde's reforms were blocked by the opposition parties and disillusion was fragmenting his own party too. In an effort to continue civilian government all the parties agreed that Belaunde should rule for sixty days by decree. Many valuable and urgent reforms were tackled. But unwisely Belaunde used his power to make a settlement with the International Petroleum Company (a subsidiary of Standard Oil of New Jersey), resolving long-standing disagreements about mining rights, in a manner which many of his closest supporters interpreted as a 'sell out' to

American oil interests. At this point the army, which had been waiting openly in the wings, assumed power.

General Velasco was little known outside army circles. He came from a lower-middle-class family and rose through the ranks. Nationalism and a strong dislike for the oligarchy seem to dominate his thinking. Within a few months of the coup those generals holding ministerial appointments who were more conservative were replaced by 'Nasserites'. Backing the generals was the Centro de Altos Estudos Militares, which, though a military training centre, actively hammered out policies of reform. The Peruvian military can, in addition, claim closer contact with the peasantry than can most of the politicians. Many officers have served in remote Indian areas; and annually the army discharges thousands of young men to whom it has taught literacy and skills; the army has co-operated in programmes of road building and agricultural extension.

In the first few months of power the military rulers attacked corruption, tax evasion and loose morality with puritan vigour. The captured guerrilla leaders were tried and sentenced. Political activity was banned in the universities. The assets of the I.P.C. were confiscated; Peruvian fishing rights up to 200 miles from the coast were claimed and enforced; indigenous banks were controlled and the nationalization of foreign banks announced. Diplomatic relations were established with East European communist countries. After this flurry of radical measures it seemed as if the impetus to reform was declining and that the generals would soon restore civilian rule. Then, in June 1969, General Velasco announced his measures for land reform and made it clear that the military would stay in power until these had been achieved.

The keynote of these reforms is their thoroughness. Belaunde's government had redistributed some inefficiently farmed land, allotting it to small farmers. The new reforms expropriated even the efficient, wealthy and often foreign-owned sugar estates, turning them into co-operatives managed by the same personnel who worked for the former landowner. Nevertheless estate-owners have been allowed to retain substantial farms for themselves. Confiscated farms are sold to credit-worthy farmers. Programmes of education and technical assistance are planned to reduce the inefficiency of the very small farms. In abolishing the latifundia the purpose of the reforms is to develop efficient medium and small independent peasant holdings.

These reforms are being carried out with military speed and efficiency – but over the heads of the peasantry. How far can the social structure be changed without active co-operation from below? How far will political parties be able to exploit either local grievances or the growing self-awareness of the peasantry to restore their popular support. The measures attacking United States' economic interests were highly popular; yet the military rulers have done little to harm business interests in Peru, have not in fact controlled foreign banks, and have made an agreement with United States' interests for the exploitation of copper deposits. Their policy of economic development rests heavily on foreign private investment even while emphasis is placed on the assistance to be given to local enterprises.

Cuba

Cuba has experienced a revolution – in the sense that Fidel Castro's assumption of power was by violent means and that his government has attempted to radically alter the social structure of the country. Why did this occur in Cuba? It is one of the wealthiest among the poorer nations which we have been discussing and Castro's victory seems almost incredible after his earlier heroic but disastrous attempts to win support and power.

Cuba's *per-capita* income in the 1950s was two or three times higher than that of countries such as Peru and Colombia – it approximated to that of Greece, for instance. As a result, social services were far more developed; over a third of the children of school age attended school and only a quarter of the adult population was illiterate. Yet the Cuban income was only a fifth of that of the United States, so close a neighbour and example; it was even markedly lower than that obtaining in the southern states of the United States. In spite of its relative affluence Cuba shared the characteristics common to the poorer nations. With its economy dominated by sugar it was heavily dependent upon the United States. United States' investments in Cuba were exceeded in Latin America only in Venezuela and Brazil. Much of the land was in large, foreign-owned sugar estates and locally owned cattle ranches; much of the land was under-used; high unemployment rates inhibited the introduction of mechanized farming. Most of the peasant farmers had small plots – but not so small as in other Latin American states. A high proportion of the rural population was however not peasants but labourers on the estates, often working for only a few months of the year. A quarter of the total labour force was employed in the sugar industry.

One fifth of the island's population lived in Havana though the industrial potential was very undeveloped. Nevertheless the industrial workers were relatively well paid and, compared with the rural workers, highly organized in trade unions.

Most writers refer to the stagnation suffered in the Cuban economy from the 1920s onwards. In thirty years, Cuba's *per-capita* income had fallen from one third of that of the United States to one fifth. A smaller proportion of children attended school. Nearly a fifth of the labour force was in the 1950s unemployed with a like proportion seriously under-employed; two thirds of the working population was earning less than £30 a month. During the 1950s little change in these conditions was experienced, any rise in national income being absorbed by the rapidly rising population.

In June 1952, a presidential election was to be held. One of the candidates was Fulgencio Batista who as military leader behind the scenes and as president had dominated Cuban politics for two decades. A public opinion poll in March showed him to be trailing behind two other candidates; he took control of the armed forces and again assumed the reins of government. His action was soon challenged in the courts as violating the constitution, by a twenty-six-year-old lawyer, Fidel Castro. Castro was the son of a relatively wealthy Spanish immigrant sugar farmer but he grew up in the countryside on the estate, schooling first in Santiago and then in Havana. At the university, Castro was politically active and in 1947 joined a small force which planned to invade the Dominican Republic and overthrow President Trujillo. He married a fellow-student from a conservative family. After graduating he built up a busy practice, largely in defending farmers, workers and political prisoners. He stood for Congress in the abortive 1952 election.

Castro's appeal to the courts against Batista was rejected and he decided that the government could only be overthrown by violent means. He organized a small force of two hundred men, mostly students or university graduates and on 26 July 1953 attacked the country's second largest military barracks – Fort Moncada in Santiago. The assault failed, many of the men were killed and the remaining few, such as Fidel Castro and his brother Raul, were captured. The incident led to stringently repressive measures from the Batista government – mass executions and censorship. Castro was tried in the courts and in the course of his defence made his famous 'history will absolve me' speech. He cited the plight of not only the urban and rural workers but also of the professional middle strata – teachers who were badly paid, professionals with university degrees who could not find work, small businessmen hit by the country's economic stagnation. He stated that his government would cleanse the country of corruption, industrialize it, grant ownership of their farms to those who had previously rented them, redistribute the land of the estates to the peasants and assist the latter to farm efficiently through co-operatives and technical aid. Housing rents would be halved. Just as every peasant should own his land so every family should own its own home. Such proposals have, however, been advocated by numerous popular leaders of Latin America – whose subsequent reforms, if they achieved power, were relatively mild. The ruling oligarchies can, without greatly jeopardizing their own position, create a rural society of small peasant farmers which itself is seen as contributing to the future stability of the country.

Castro was gaoled, receiving a fifteen-year sentence; but such was Batista's growing unpopularity that he announced an amnesty and Castro was freed in May 1955. He had become a popular hero, but rather than try to organize opposition to Batista within Cuba he went to Mexico and, with other exiles, began to organize a new rebel force. In November 1956, eighty-two armed men set off in a boat designed for a fraction of that number. In their delays they failed to co-ordinate with risings within Cuba; eventually they landed on 2 December and, within days, most of the rebels were killed or captured. Fidel Castro and eleven others managed to make their way to hiding in the highest peaks of the Sierra Maestra.

Over the next two years, from this seemingly hopeless position, Castro developed his guerrilla movement which was to bring him to power. Subsequent eulogies have stressed peasant participation in the movement; but it seems unlikely that any large numbers were under arms. The peasants initially gave refuge to Castro men, then supplied them and ultimately found it less dangerous to aid the guerrillas than the government forces. Significantly, Castro's men did not pillage and rape, as did so many guerrilla bands; they paid for supplies and taught the peasants. Land reforms were quickly carried out in conquered areas. In February 1958 the 'rebel radio' began broadcasting from 'the territory of Free Cuba in the Sierra Maestra'; this undoubtedly encouraged resistance to Batista in the rest of the country. Sabotage increased in the urban areas. But a general strike called in the spring of 1958 was a failure, partly through the ineptitude of its leaders, partly because troops were quickly brought in to crush it. The Cuban communist party had consistently failed to support Castro, maintaining that he was an adventurer and that the government could only be overthrown by a rising of urban workers; it supported him only when his strength was manifestly undiminished by the strike.

The Cuban army was 30,000 strong and during the period of guerrilla warfare was fully stretched maintaining order in the towns and throughout the country. In May 1958, with growing opposition to his brutality and corruption, Batista ordered a full-scale offensive against Castro. But even though the guerrillas had rarely had more than 300 men under arms the attacks failed; the humane treatment of captured troops increased disillusion in the Cuban army and after a few swift moves in which the guerrillas bisected the island and captured strategic points, the army surrendered. Batista fled though not before he tried in vain to install a new military junta. He obviously had almost no support within Cuba and towards the end of 1958 had, furthermore, lost the support of the U.S. government which ceased to supply him with arms.

In mid 1958, on the threshold of victory, Castro had rejected proposals for a united front which threatened in effect to maintain the political power of the ruling oligarchy and the army, even if Batista were sacrificed. Yet the government which he first set up had a strong 'liberal' flavour and it was only during the ensuing months that Castro became an apparent Marxist and communist. Two factors seem responsible for this change. Within Cuba it became obvious that if the reforms originally postulated were to be taken to their logical conclusion, the structural change in the society would be quite radical; the upper strata were thus alienated and emigrated; Castro relied therefore more specifically upon the workers and peasants whose support he undoubtedly had. Secondly, with the increasing U.S. opposition to the regime and the final rupture of all relationships, Cuba was thrown into dependency upon the U.S.S.R.

This is not the place in which to evaluate the success of the Castro regime; the people are still poor, though no worse off than in 1950. Nor can we comment upon the tactics, correct or otherwise, employed in attempting to achieve the stated goals. What is important is the nature of those goals and the difference between these goals and those, for example, of the military regime in Peru.

In the first place, Castro has created a far more egalitarian society. Not only have rents been reduced as promised in the 1953 manifesto, but the whole wage structure has been altered so that the best paid professionals such as doctors earn only five or six times as much as the worker with a minimum wage. A shortage of consumer goods serves to reduce even further the gap in styles of living between the upper and lower strata. Secondly, and as a consequence of the above, the distinction between urban affluence and rural poverty is being eliminated. Rural wages have been equated with those of industry, and in many respects the rural worker is now better off. Schools and other services have been provided in the remoter areas where they were previously lacking, so that people of these parts may enjoy the same opportunities for social mobility as those elsewhere. Urban workers now help with the sugar harvest as a civic duty. The migration into Havana has been halted and, bereft of its rich upper classes, the city appears quiet and decaying in comparison with its former glamour.

These changes have been effected substantially through the activities of the Institute of Agrarian Reform (I. N. R. A.) – throughout the 1960s one of the most powerful organs of the government.

From an earlier reliance on individual, owner-operated holdings, Castro's policy shifted towards an emphasis on collectivized holdings. The sugar estates and large ranches were appropriated as state farms; their workers continued in employment but under better conditions with higher wages and employment guaranteed throughout the year. Peasants gained title to the land which they farmed and shared in the redistribution of land from those estates which were broken up. But their activities have become increasingly subject to government planning, control and assistance. The farmer is no longer reliant solely upon his own labour, for brigades work in turn on the land of each member.

Throughout the decade the government, through the radio and press and through a number of quasi-political associations, has striven with considerable success to awaken the political consciousness of the masses. Land reform has not been seen merely as a means of pacifying the peasantry but also of incorporating them fully into national life.

Tanzania

Julius Nyerere, President of Tanzania, is pledged to create a socialist and egalitarian society by means of deliberate and peaceful planned change. He argues that violence is unnecessary for the elements of the new society are present in the traditional social structures of the Tanzanian peoples; the task is to avoid taking the roads leading either to capitalism or to the authoritarian socialist state (as exemplified in eastern Europe) with their respective attendant evils.

Tanzania is one of the poorest of the under-developed nations of the world, its people having a *per capita* annual income of only £25. Its population of twelve million is widely dispersed through an area larger than France and the two Germanys. Road and rail communications are poorly developed. The principal export crop, sisal (accounting for a quarter of the country's exports), is grown in foreign-owned plantations on the coast. The second most important export, coffee, is grown by individual peasant farmers, notably the Chagga, living on the slopes of Mt Kilimanjaro. Cotton, too, is produced by peasants. There is relatively little exploitation of mineral wealth, diamonds from the south being the principal export. Poverty, with colonial rule, combined to stultify the development of secondary and post-secondary education. On the eve of Independence in 1961 there were only 4,000 pupils in secondary schools – the majority of these being in the lowest forms. There were less than a hundred Tanzanian university graduates. Of the small number of graduates teaching in Tanzanian secondary schools, only fifteen – an eighth of the total – were African. Only 430 Tanzanians were studying outside their own country – a half of these being at Makerere University College in Uganda.

Ethnically the population of Tanzania is diverse. On the coast a mixed African and Arab stock is popularly designated as Arab, the term reinforced by their adherence to Islam. In the interior are Nilotic, Nilo-Hamitic and Bantu peoples. Well over one hundred distinct ethnic groups are said to exist. But no one of these is large enough to dominate the country. Nor, in the pre-colonial period, were there any large kingdoms in a position to dominate neighbouring peoples. Though some of the larger ethnic groups each recognized a shared culture, they were usually politically organized in small chiefdoms and it was only in the colonial period that they grouped themselves into a federation and, in some cases, created a paramount chieftaincy. Set against this diversity is the unifying factor of Swahili language and culture. Swahili was carried throughout the country in the pre-colonial period by the 'Arab' slavers; subsequently it was largely used as the language of colonial administration. Today it has been recognized as the national language and is a compulsory subject in all secondary schools. Politicians must address their local rallies in Swahili, using interpreters where necessary, in this way identifying themselves with the national culture rather than with the local ethnic group.

Although Tanzania's attainment of independence was almost without violent incident, in the early years of German colonial rule her people had mounted some impressive resistance movements – especially the Maji Maji revolt of 1905. This had united many ethnic groups and the mythology which subsequently developed was used to foster unity in the independence movement. In the British colonial period the Tanganyikan African Association was founded in the 1920s by educated civil servants and traders, more as a social than a political association; its influence was limited to the urban areas. But after 1945, it gradually developed into a nationalist movement and extended its interest to the rural areas. At the same time 'tribal unions', led predominantly by literate and prosperous local citizens, were developing in many ethnic groups and campaigning against specific incidents of colonial or chiefly rule. Between the T.A.A. and these unions there frequently existed a symbiotic relationship as each enlisted the support of the other to enhance its own strength and claims. Julius Nyerere, son of a chief of a small ethnic group on the shore of Lake Victoria was educated successively at one of his country's leading secondary schools, Makerere and at the University of Edinburgh, where he received his M.A. He returned to Tanganyika in 1952 and renewed his activity in the T.A.A.; he became its President in 1953. In 1954 at a meeting called to consider the constitution of the T.A.A., the Tanganyika African National Union was formed. This became the dominant political party in the country and in 1960 formed a responsible government with Nyerere as Chief Minister. With Independence, he became Prime Minister and, a year later, President.

T.A.N.U. became the sole party in Tanzania more by default than by design. In its early years it sought the support of Asians and Europeans who voted on separate electoral rolls. The chiefs formed no focus of opposition; most of them were influential only in their local areas; the tardy development of the native authority system had not enabled them to recognize their common interest; and in many ancephalous societies men were appointed to office who had little traditional claim to authority – they were the classic 'straw chiefs' with minimal local prestige. Again, among the western educated élite were several who couched their policies in terms far more radical and Marxist than those used by Nyerere; yet direct confrontations seem to have been avoided and the 'rebels' have lost influence. Partly because of the numerical weakness of ethnic groups and the deliberate policy of disassociating politicians from their groups and from their interest associations, opposition groups have not been able to develop successfully a basis of power to be used against incumbent office-holders.

President Nyerere is, in his country, referred to as *Mwalimu* – the teacher, or *Baba Ya Taifa* – father of the nation. In the ideology which he has propounded the key term is *Ujamaa* – family hood or brotherhood. Nyerere believes that the bonds of community, inherent in traditional African society, are not necessarily incompatible with economic development and should be preserved wherever possible. These ideals form the basis of his concept of African socialism. This appeal to the traditional structure of African society legitimizes the ideology; but such is the variety of traditional structures among the varying ethnic groups that it is impossible to elaborate the nature of communal relationships or specify how they might be used in furthering economic development. In the years before 1965 the ideology of *Ujamaa* was not formulated with great precision – it was thus used to mobilize both the literate and the non-literate masses (to the extent that they were aware of it) in the cause of Independence.

While T.A.N.U. is seen, on the one hand, as the instrument for mobilizing the mass of the peasantry, the leaders have, on the other hand, been concerned to maintain its democratic nature. Thus by the standards of most single party regimes it is relatively weak at the centre. Local T.A.N.U. branches developed, as often as not from pre-existing T.A.A. branches or from ethnic associations. To a large extent they have been the creation of local leaders – the literates, wealthy traders and the like. In a country offering so few opportunities for entrepreneurship or clerical office, the party has been seen as an avenue to prestige and power. Frequently the actions of local branches have been at variance with central directives. T.A.N.U. has been overwhelmingly successful at the polls in all elections but in the late 1950s and early 1960s the proportion of the electorate which actually voted was very small. In the 1965 elections two T.A.N.U. candidates stood in each constituency and many of the incumbent members of parliament, some ministers included, were unseated.

In the 1960s attempts have been made to strengthen T.A.N.U. as an instrument of mobilization. In addition to organizational reforms, two events are important. In 1962–3 chiefs were removed as officials in the native authority system though many of the more able men found administrative and executive posts in the new structures of local government. By this move the focus of local administration shifted from the traditional office-holders to T.A.N.U. In January 1964 a large section of the army mutinied, the principal demands being for higher pay and swifter Africanization of the officer cadres. Strategic buildings were seized, most of the leading politicians went into hiding and looting broke out in Dar es Salaam. British commandos restored control and the mutinying battalions were subsequently disbanded; Nigerian troops maintained order until a new army was created, much more closely associated with the party; in fact it was at first suggested that the T.A.N.U. youth league should provide the nucleus of the new army. Instead a form of National Service was instituted; men worked for instance on community projects in the rural areas, or if university graduates, as teachers, but throughout this period of service were subject to quasimilitary discipline. While these situations have undoubtedly strengthened the party, the paucity of educated men and the continued emphasis on local democracy have inhibited centralizing tendencies.

The Arusha Declaration of February 1967 and the subsequent pronouncements in the same vein must be seen against the background of the social and economic changes of the previous decade. The enrolment in secondary schools doubled between 1961 and 1966. In 1960 a university college opened in Dar es Salaam and in 1966 the country had nearly two thousand university students. The drift to the big cities and the rising unemployment there began to be marked in Tanzania as in other poor countries. With the increasing size of the educated élite the gap in living styles between this group and the mass of the people became more obvious. One factor which probably precipitated the Arusha declaration was the refusal of the university students in Dar es Salaam to carry out their National Service tasks at rates of pay lower than those usually awarded to men with their educational qualifications; it was assumed that they were unwilling to place themselves at the service of the community which had financed their education.

Economic development made little progress. Agricultural schemes of a wide variety were attempted but very few were successful; a few emphasized collective farming but most depended heavily on government capital and personnel – all too often lacking. Foreign aid was minimal – effectively amounting to 8s per head per annum when loan repayments are deducted. Aid from West Germany was forfeited when the Tanzanian government recognized East Germany, and from Britain when Tanzania broke off relations consequent upon the O.A.U. resolution on Rhodesia.

The Arusha Declaration propounds an ideology which is rare in the poorer nations. Non-material objectives are given priority over material ones; in other words it is not the aim of the country to reach western living standards as quickly as possible. Instead 'traditional' values are stressed and in particular that of equality. The avowed policy of the government is to prevent the development of social stratification as it occurs in the industrial nations. To achieve this the emphasis is placed on self-reliance; at the national level a reduced dependence upon foreign aid; and since this means forgoing a policy of rapid industrialization, the improvement in living standards must come from development in the rural areas, the stress again being placed upon community self-help rather than government assistance. The agents in guiding and changing the values of the people are to be the schools and the *ujamaa* villages.

The *ujamaa* villages are collective or co-operative enterprises. Joint decision-making is emphasized and economic inequality between individuals minimized; in particular one man may not hire the labour of another and the growth of a category of wealthy farmers is prevented. It is hoped that conditions – both material and non-material – in these villages will be such that the drift to the towns is halted. (In the meantime unemployed in the cities are periodically rounded up and repatriated, while from some rural areas a permit is needed, in theory, to move to the city.)

The schools of Tanzania inherited from the colonial period are élitist in outlook. Instead they must train the youth for service to the community and recognize, in particular, that most of those leaving primary school will work on the land. Higher education too, must stress service rather than individual reward.

The aims of the Tanzanian government are set out in these policy pronouncements in the most general terms. Translating them into action is a harder task. Most of the successful agricultural development, coffee growing, for instance, has been through individual initiative; it is often the wealthy farmers who are able to experiment and raise outputs per man hour or per acre. Many techniques which might raise production may be incompatible with the type of collective farming envisaged in the *ujamaa* villages, with their emphasis on traditional, rather than new, social relationships. Again, many of those in positions of local leadership, sometimes even T.A.N.U. officials, may as wealthy farmers or literates be out of sympathy with the egalitarian ideals of the national leaders. The transformation of the ideology enshrined in the educational system is bound to be slow and difficult when all those now available as teachers have been indoctrinated by the existing system. The attempts to bridge the gap between the educated élite and the masses have been of a symbolic nature only. Ministers and senior civil servants took 20 per cent and 10 per cent salary cuts respectively in 1966 and the former gave up their opulent government-owned Mercedes. Party officials at all levels were forbidden to own shares or lease property. But the colonial salary structure is basically maintained and the educated élite seem likely to ensure that their own children enjoy a similar status. Observers detect a lack of enthusiasm among the educated élite for the full implications of the Arusha Declaration; nor does it seem likely that much pressure for its full implementation will come from the masses. As it is said with irony in Dar es Salaam, the question here is not 'can one have socialism in one country?' but 'can one have socialism with one socialist?' Obviously the tenets of the Arusha Declaration cannot transform Tanzania overnight; clearly they aim to create a society very different from that which is developing in other African nations; but will the political leaders be able to control the direction of change so that their country moves towards *ujamaa* rather than towards increasing social inequality and political unrest?

One could extend these vignettes both in number and length, for me to do so is beyond the scope of this book but I hope that I have interested some readers sufficiently to encourage them to make their own analyses. I have tried in these pages to outline some of the variables which I consider to be significant. One cannot produce a generalized picture of the social structure of poorer nations; each has its own peculiarities stemming from its historical past, the nature of its economic development and the sequence of recent social changes. Thus, for example, I have argued that the weak development of class consciousness derives, in part, from the workers' lack of commitment to their trade unions; this in turn is due to poor union leadership, an ill-educated and often transient work force, dependence on patronage for social advancement and on ethnic associations for social security; yet these factors do not always operate with similar effect and in some countries trade unions are a much stronger political force than in others.

Again, I have restricted myself to a narrow framework of analysis – focusing the discussion on the emergent patterns of social stratification in the poorer nations – the new social groupings among peasants, urban workers and the educated élite and the relationships between these. The day-to-day events in these nations ought to be seen as the outcome of these relationships – rather than as the result of clashes of personality, so often the stand-by of ill-informed journalists. Yet other factors must not be ignored. For instance social changes take place within an environment of economic and social resources. Nigeria's recent history cannot be isolated from the sudden wealth from oil – wealth which filters through many channels to the masses and which governs Nigeria's relationships with the western powers. We must not see the educated élites of a country solely as groups competing for power. In his speech to the nation in July 1970 Fidel Castro announced that Cuba had not only failed to reach the (rather high) target of 10 million tons of sugar, but that other areas of the economy had been deprived as resources were diverted to the sugar harvest. He attributed the cause of the failure to poor planning, organizational inefficiency and ignorance on the part of the political leaders. Similarly the success of Tanzania in achieving a socialist state will depend heavily on the number and ability of men available for implementing the proposed reforms from the level of the state to the smallest village. But important as these facts are they too cannot be considered in isolation – though many aid-giving agencies do so in promoting schemes to increase wealth or teach new skills without considering the impact on the social structure and its consequent changes.

The disciples of Marx and Lenin, of Mao Tse Tung and Che Guevara debate the revolutionary role of the peasants, urban workers and party. The lessons of these pages are that, confined to a theoretical plane, these discussions are likely to be sterile. The outcome in a revolutionary situation can only be predicted, if at all, with a detailed knowledge of the characteristics of the peasantry, workers and party involved. Our task is to sharpen our understanding of these varying factors.

Notes

CHAPTER 1

1. T. S. Epstein, *Economic Development and Social Change in South India*, 1962, Manchester; Manchester University Press.

2. E. R. Wolf, *Peasant Wars of the Twentieth Century*, 1969, New York: Harper & Row.

3. P. Mayer, *Townsmen or Tribesmen*, 1961, Capetown: Oxford University Press.

CHAPTER 2

1. M. M. Green, *Ibo Village Affairs*, 1947, London: Sidgwick & Jackson. For a description of another Ibo community by an Ibo social anthropologist, see V. C. Vchendu, *The Ibo of South-eastern Nigeria*, 1965, New York: Holt, Rinehart & Winston.

2. A. Beteille, *Class, Status and Power: Changing Patterns of Stratification in a Tanjore Village*, 1965, Berkeley: University of California Press.

3. A. R. Holmberg, 'Changing community attitudes and values in Peru; a case study in guided change', in R. N. Adams *et al., Social Change in Latin America today*, 1960, New York: Harper Bros. M. C. Vazquez,' Changes in the stratification of an Andean hacienda', in D. B. Heath and R. N. Adams (eds.), *Contemporary cultures and Societies of Latin America*, 1965, New York: Random House.

CHAPTER 3

1. G. Rosen, *Democracy and Economic Change in India*, 1966, Berkeley: California University Press.

CHAPTER 4

1. L. Barnes, *African Renaissance*, 1969, London: Gollancz.

2. A. G. Frank, *Latin America: underdevelopment or revolution*, 1969, New York: Monthly Review Press. This volume contains a seminal essay published earlier – 'Sociology of development and underdevelopment of sociology', *Catalyst*, Summer 1967.

3. D. Lerner, 'Comparative analysis of processes of modernization' in H. Miner (ed.), *The City in Modern Africa*, 1967, London: Pall Mall Press, p. 21.

4. Lerner, op. cit., p. 22.

5. Lerner, ibid.

6. T. Parsons, *Societies: Evolutionary and Comparative Perspectives*, 1966, Englewood Cliffs: Prentice-Hall.

7. A. Sampson, *The Anatomy of Britain*, 1962, London: Hodder & Stoughton.

8. W. W. Rostow, *Stages of Economic Growth*, 1960, Cambridge University Press.

9. Lerner, op. cit., p. 25.

10. Lerner, ibid.

11. Frank, op cit., p. 56.

12. D. C. McClelland, *The Achieving Society*, 1961, New York: Free Press; D. C. McClelland, *et al.*, *Motivating Economic Development*, 1969, New York: Free Press. E. E. Hagen, *On the Theory of Social Change*, 1962, Homewood: Dorsey.

13. R. H. Dix, *Colombia: The Political Dimensions of Change*, 1967, New Haven: Yale University Press, p. 52.

14. J. D. Bernal, *The Freedom of Necessity*, 1949: Routledge & Kegan Paul.

15. L. Althusser, 'Contradiction and overdetermination', *New Left Review*, 41, 1967.

CHAPTER 5

1. T. S. Epstein, *Economic Development and Social Change in South India*, 1962, Manchester: Manchester University Press.

2. Epstein, op. cit., p. 193.

3. Epstein, op. cit., p. 53.

4. E. Wolf, 'On peasant rebellions' *New Society* 362, 4 September 1969, p. 351.

5. E. Wolf, ibid.

6. Wolf, op. cit., p. 353.

7. Wolf, ibid.

8. Barrington Moore, *Social origins of dictatorship and democracy*, 1967, London: Allen Lane, The Penguin Press, pp. 380–85.

9. R. Patch, 'Bolivia: U.S. assistance in a revolutionary setting', in R. N. Adams *et al.*, *Social Change in Latin America Today*, 1960, New York: Harper Bros.

10. G. Rosen, *Democracy and Economic Change in India*, 1966, Berkeley: California University Press, pp. 145–6.

CHAPTER 6

1. D. N. Majumdar, *Social Contours of an Industrial City*, 1960 Bombay: Asia Publishing House.

2. R. Mukerjee and B. Singh, *A district town in transition: social and economic survey of Gorakhpur*, 1965, London: Asia Publishing House.

3. L. R. Peattie, *The View from the 'Barrio'*, 1968, Ann Arbor: University of Michigan Press, pp. 13–16.

4. *Report of the commission on the review of wages, salaries and conditions of service of the junior employees of the governments of the Federation and in private establishments, 1963–4*. (The Morgan Commission), 1964, Lagos: Federal Ministry of Information, p. 13.

5. F. A. Wells and W. A. Warmington, *Studies in Industrialization: Nigeria and the Cameroons*, 1962, London: Oxford University Press.

6. Majumdar, op. cit., p. 144.

7. B. V. Shah, 'Inequality of educational opportunities: a case study', *Economic Weekly*, 20 August 1960.

8. P. Mayer, *Townsmen or Tribesmen*, 1961, Capetown: Oxford University Press.

9. Mayer, op. cit., p. 284.

10. Mayer, op. cit., p. 285.

11. Mayer, op. cit., p. 284.

12. Mayer, op. cit., p. 285.

13. C. Achebe, *No Longer at Ease*, 1960, London: Heinemann.

14. W. P. Mangin, 'The role of regional associations in the adaptation of rural migrants to cities in Peru', in D. P. Heath and R. N. Adams, op. cit.

15. L. I. and S. H. Rudolph, *The Modernity of Tradition*, 1967, Chicago: Chicago University Press, p. 35.

16. Rudolph and Rudolph, op. cit., p. 47.

17. Rudolph and Rudolph, op. cit., pp. 72–3.

18. N. R. Sheth, *The Social Framework of an Indian Factory*, 1968, Bombay: Oxford University Press.

19. Sheth, op. cit., p. 123.

20. M. Weiner, *The Politics of Scarcity*, 1962, Chicago: Chicago University Press, p. 197.

21. Weiner, op. cit., pp. 213–14.

CHAPTER 7

1. See B. Prasad, *The Indian Administrative Service*, 1968, Delhi: S. Chand; and W. H. Morris-Jones, *The Government and Politics of India*, 2nd ed. 1967, London: Hutchinson.

2. L. I. and S. H. Rudolph, 'The political modernization of an Indian feudal order', *Social Forces* 4, 1968.

3. P. R. Brass, cited in T. Bottomore, 'Cohesion and Division in Indian Elites', in P. Mason (ed.), *India and Ceylon : Unity and Diversity*, 1967, London: Oxford University Press, p. 247.

4. Bottomore, op. cit., pp. 244–5.

5. R. H. Dix, *Colombia : The Political Dimensions of Change*, 1967, New Haven: Yale University Press, p. 342.

6. F. Bourricaud, *Power in Society in Contemporary Peru*, 1970, London: Faber, pp. 46–7.

7. Dix, op. cit., p. 49.

8. V. L. Fluharty, cited in Dix, op. cit., p. 62.

9. A. R. Desai, *The Social background of Indian Nationalism*, 1966, Bombay: Popular Prakashan.

10. R. Bendix, *Nation building and citizenship*, 1964, New York: Wiley, p. 241.

11. R. Segal, *The Crisis of India*, 1965, London: Penguin Books, p. 258.

12. S. Harrison, *India, the most Dangerous Decades*, 1960, Princeton: Princeton University Press, p. 178.

13. Harrison, op. cit., pp. 180–81.

14. Harrison, op. cit., p. 180.

15. Harrison, op. cit., p. 182.

16. Harrison, op. cit., p. 180.

17. C. Achebe, *Man of the People*, 1966, London: Heinemann.

CHAPTER 8

1. C. Johnson, *Revolutionary Change*, 1968, London: University of London Press.

2. R. H. Dix, *Colombia : The Political Dimensions of Change*, 1967, Newhaven: Yale University Press, pp. 360–61.

3. Dix, op. cit., p. 50.

4. Dix, op. cit., p. 98.

5. Dix, op. cit., p. 168.

6. Dix, op. cit., p. 360.

For Further Reading

The literature on the poorer nations is vast and rapidly increasing. In the foregoing pages I have provided footnote references to a few works which I have used, and often quoted from, extensively. Many of these I should certainly recommend to the reader who wishes to pursue further any of the themes which I have briefly touched. In the following note I not only refer again to those books, but have added a few others which should be useful in provoking further discussion.

THE THEORY OF SOCIAL CHANGE

To the reader who wishes to see how social scientists have interpreted the processes of social change I would first recommend an excellent reader – A. and E. Etzioni (eds.), *Social Change* (1964, New York: Basic Books). A structural viewpoint is represented by T. Parsons, *Societies: Evolutionary and Comparative Perspectives* (1966, Englewood Cliffs: Prentice-Hall), while D. Lerner, *The Passing of Traditional Society: Modernising the Middle East* (1958, Glencoe: Free Press) has had a substantial impact on studies made in the past decade or so. Highly critical of these approaches are I. L. Horowitz, *Three Worlds of Development* (1966, New York: Oxford University Press) and A. G. Frank, *Latin America: Underdevelopment or Revolution* (1969, New York: Monthly Review Press).

In these pages I have taken social stratification as a unifying thread for my argument. Two excellent readers provide background reading – C. S. Heller, *Structured Social Inequality* (1969, New York: Macmillan) and A. Beteille (ed.), *Social Inequality* (1969, London: Penguin Books). The editor of the first-mentioned work has provided her own introduction to the various sections of her reader, in which she criticizes the contributions contained in the extracts quoted. Beteille's book is useful in that it covers non-western societies to a degree unusual in works of this kind.

It has not been my task to do more than indicate the economic dependency of the poorer nations upon the industrial western nations.

A good introduction to the economic problems of the former is: J. Bhagwati, *The Economics of Underdeveloped Countries* (1966, London: Weidenfeld & Nicolson), or for a more controversial presentation, P. Baran, *The Political Economy of Growth* (1962, New York: Monthly Review Press). The Pearson Report, published at the close of the United Nations First Development Decade, discusses the role of the industrial nations in the development of the poorer nations: Lester B. Pearson (Chairman), *Partners in Development: Report of the Committee on International Development* (1970, New York: Praeger).

REGIONAL STUDIES

To the reader who wishes to explore in greater depth a single continent or country I make the following suggestions.

Africa: For general introduction to continent, P. van den Berghe (ed.), *Africa: Social Problems of Change and Conflict* (1965, San Francisco: Chandler Publishing Company) is an admirable reader. P. C. Lloyd, *Africa in Social Change* (1967, London: Penguin Books) confines its description to West Africa though the themes discussed are applicable in general terms throughout tropical Africa. Almost every African state has now been described in a monograph by a political scientist; the three following countries illustrate Africa's diversity:

Nigeria: J. S. Coleman, *Nigeria: Background to Nationalism* (1958, Berkeley: University of California Press) covers the rise of the Nationalist Movement; K. W. J. Post, *The Nigerian Federal Election of 1959* (1963, London: Oxford University Press), and R. L. Sklar, *Nigerian Political Parties* (1963, Princeton: Princeton University Press) deal with political parties and elections of the period around 1960; B. J. Dudley, *Parties and Politics in Northern Nigeria* (1968, London: Frank Cass), and C. S. Whitaker, *The Politics of Tradition: Continuity and Change in Northern Nigeria* (1970, Princeton: Princeton University Press) describe northern Nigeria in greater depth. J. P. Mackintosh, *Nigerian Government and Politics* (1966, London: Allen & Unwin) gives a general account of the Nigerian political scene which an account by a journalist – W. Schwarz, *Nigeria* (1968, London: Pall Mall Press) extends to the mid 1960s. K. S. Panter-Brick (ed.), *Nigerian Politics and Military Rule* (1970, London: University of London Press) describes the events leading up to the 1966 coup and military rule.

Ghana : D. E. Apter, *The Gold Coast in Transition* (1955, Princeton: Princeton University Press), and D. Austin, *Politics in Ghana 1946–1960* (1964, London: Oxford University Press) together deal with the political history of the pre- and immediate post-independence periods. An analysis from a radical viewpoint of the coup which deposed Nkrumah is provided by B. Fitch and M. Oppenheimer, *Ghana : End of an Illusion* (1966, New York: Monthly Review Press), while one of the leading actors has provided his own version: A. A. Arifa, *The Ghana Coup* (1966, London: Frank Cass). H. L. Bretton, *The Rise and Fall of Kwame Nkrumah* (1967. London: Pall Mall Press) is an account less biased by theoretical preconceptions or personal involvement.

Tanzania : The attempts of Nyerere to create a socialist state are too recent for the published works of scholars to have judged their effect. The antecedent situation is covered by G. A. Maguire, *Toward 'Uhuru' in Tanzania* (1969, Cambridge: Cambridge University Press) and H. Bienen, *Tanzania: Party Transformation and Economic Development* (1967, Princeton: Princeton University Press). The hopes and ideals embodied in the Arusha Declaration are set forth in Nyerere's own words: J. K. Nyerere, *Ujamaa : Essays in Socialism* (1968, Dar es Salaam: Oxford University Press).

India : G. Myrdal, *Asian Drama : An Enquiry into the Poverty of Nations* (1968, London: Allen Lane The Penguin Press) is a vast survey of the problems of India and her neighbours. Much shorter, though no less provocative, is R. Segal, *The Crisis of India* (1965, London: Penguin Books).

Several works give an excellent coverage of specific themes. Thus G. Rosen, *Democracy and Economic Change in India* (1966, Berkeley: University of California Press) is useful in describing economic changes as they affect the urban worker and rural peasant. L. I. and S. H. Rudolph, *The Modernity of Tradition* (1967, Chicago: University of Chicago Press) has good sections on caste associations and the ideology of Gandhi. S. Harrison, *India, the Most Dangerous Decades* (1960, Princeton: Princeton University Press) discusses both the influence and effectiveness of the communist parties, and linguistic issues. M. Weiner, *The Politics of Scarcity* (1962, Chicago: University of Chicago Press) deals successively with associations and organizations of various types – trade unions, student and agrarian movements, etc., while a symposium P. Mason (ed.), *India and Ceylon : Unity and Diversity* (1967, London: Oxford University Press) has valuable contributions on castes and élites.

Latin America : Seminal articles are contained in a number of symposia and readers, for instance: C. Veliz (ed.), *Latin America and the Caribbean: A Handbook* (1968, London: Anthony Blond); C. Veliz (ed.) *Obstacles to Change in Latin America* (1965, London: Oxford University Press); C. Veliz (ed.), *The Politics of Conformity in Latin America* (1967, London: Oxford University Press); D. B. Heath and R. N. Adams, *Contemporary Cultures and Societies of Latin America* (1965, New York: Random House) and J. Petras and M. Zeitlin (eds.), *Latin America : Reform or Revolution* (1964, Greenwich: Fawcett).

Excellent monograph studies of particular countries are, for Peru: F. Bourricaud, *Power and Society in Contemporary Peru* (1970, London: Faber & Faber) and C. A. Astiz, *Pressure Groups and Power Elites in Peruvian Politics* (1969, Ithaca: Cornell University Press); and for Colombia: R. H. Dix, *Colombia : The Political Dimensions of Change* (1967, New Haven: Yale University Press) and O. Fals Borda, *Subversion and Social Change in Colombia* (1969, New York: Columbia University Press). Most of the literature on Cuba is highly partisan, but D. Seers (ed.), *Cuba : The Economic and Social Revolution* (1964, Chapel Hill: University of California Press) provides a well-balanced picture of the Cuban economy at the beginning of the 1960s, and R. E. Ruiz, *Cuba : The Making of a Revolution* (1968, Amherst: University of Massachusetts Press) gives a good historical background. L. Huberman and P. M. Sweezy, *Cuba : Anatomy of a Revolution* (1961, 2nd ed., New York: Monthly Review Press) chronicles Castro's rise to power. The situation in post-revolutionary Cuba is described by L. Huberman and P. M. Sweezy, *Socialism in Cuba* (1969, New York: Monthly Review Press), while J. Yglesias, *In the Fist of the Revolution* (1968, London: Allen Lane The Penguin Press) gives a journalist's account of life in a small country town in 1967.

THEMATIC STUDIES

Rural development : A number of studies, mostly by social anthropologists have analysed the changes in social structure consequent upon economic development. My own sample of these would include the following: F. G. Bailey, *Caste and the Economic Frontier* (1957, Manchester: Manchester University Press), T. S. Epstein, *Economic Development and Social Change in South India* (1962, Manchester: Manchester University Press), A. Beteille, *Class, Status and Power : Changing Patterns of Stratification in a Tanjore Village* (1965, Berkeley: University of California Press), R. F. Salisbury, *Vunamami : Economic Transformation in a Traditional Society* (1970, Berkeley: University of California Press), N. Long, *Social Change and the Individual* (1968,

Manchester: Manchester University Press), P. L. Doughty, *Hualyas: an Andean District in Search of Progress* (1968, Ithaca: Cornell University Press). There is of course a much larger anthropological literature oriented more towards the traditional structure of society than towards the ongoing processes of change.

Urban life: While the social anthropologist can present a holistic picture of his village community, a correspondingly scholarly description of the vast modern city is impossible. For comparison therefore we have but partial views of urban life. Africa is best represented: P. Mayer, *Townsmen or Tribesmen* (1961, Capetown: Oxford University Press) is a classic, describing the adaptation of Xhosa to life in East London; V. Pons, *Stanleyville* (1969, London: Oxford University Press) describes with minute detail the social life of Avenue 21, a street in that city. L. Plotnicov, *Strangers To The City* (1967, Pittsburgh: Pittsburgh University Press) tells, through the biographies of eight men of different ethnic groups, of their activities in Jos, Northern Nigeria. A Symposium, P. C. Lloyd, A. L. Mabogonje and B. Awe (eds.), *The City of Ibadan* (1967, London: Cambridge University Press) describes many of the facets of life in tropical Africa's largest city. In addition African city life is the subject of many of that continent's young novelists, for example, Chinua Achebe, Timothy Aluko, Cyprian Ekwensi and others whose works are published in Heinemann's *African Writers Series*.

Indian scholars have produced a large number of meticulous socio-economic surveys but studies comparable to those cited for Africa are lacking. One turns instead to the novelists, such as R. K. Narayan, for the graphic description of city life. Though somewhat weak in their sociological analysis, two books do give the reader some of the flavour of life in Latin American cities: A. H. Whiteford, *Two Cities of Latin America: A Comparative Description of Social Classes* (1964, Garden City: Doubleday), compares Popayan in Colombia with Queretaro in Mexico and L. R. Peattie, *The View from the 'Barrio'* (1968, Ann Arbor: University of Michigan Press) describes a neighbourhood of Ciudad Guayana, a steel city in Venezuela. One can hardly omit, too, the classics of Oscar Lewis in giving us the raw data of the 'culture of poverty'; thus in *Five Families* (1959, New York: Basic Books) and *The Children of Sanchez* (1962, Canada: Secker & Warburg; 1965, London: Penguin Books) he describes life in the slums of Mexico city.

The educated élite: Descriptions of the western educated élite and the ideologies espoused by them are, of course, contained in most of the political studies of individual states. Three symposia have a regional coverage: P. C. Lloyd (ed.), *The New Elites of Tropical Africa* (1966, London: Oxford University Press), E. Leach and S. N. Mukherjee, *Elites in South Asia* (1970, Cambridge: Cambridge University Press) and S. M. Lipset and A. Solari (eds.), *Elites in Latin America* (1967, New York: Oxford University Press).

A useful summary of African socialism in its various forms is contained in W. H. Friedland and C. G. Roseberg (eds.), *African Socialism* (1964, London: Oxford University Press), while A. J. Kinghoffer, *Soviet Perspectives on African Socialism* (1969, Rutherford: Fairleigh Dickinson University Press) outlines the official Russian attitude towards these ideologies. G. Ionescu and E. Gellner (eds.), *Populism: Its Meanings and National Characteristics* (1969, London: Weidenfeld & Nicolson) has interesting contributions on Africa and Latin America.

Many studies provide statistics of schools and scholars, but too few describe the processes of social mobility through the educational system. Exceptional studies which one would like to see replicated in other countries are: P. J. Foster, *Education and Social Change in Ghana* (1965, London: Routledge & Kegan Paul), and R. Clignet and P. J. Foster, *The Fortunate Few* (1966, Evanston: Northwestern University Press) the latter dealing with the Ivory Coast.

PROTEST MOVEMENTS

The theme of this book has been the tensions and violence consequent upon social development rather than the less obtrusive adaptation to new conditions which dominates current sociological literature. Too few studies seem willing to consider revolutionary change. Among theoretical works which tackle this issue are: S. P. Huntingdon, *Political Order in Changing Societies* (1968, New Haven: Yale University Press) and C. Johnson, *Revolutionary Change* (1968, London: University of London Press).

A most unusual yet immensely valuable symposium which covers protest movements of all types – pre- and post-colonial, strikes, religious movements, literary protest, etc., is R. I. Rotberg and A. A. Mazrui (eds.), *Protest and Power in Black Africa* (1970, New York: Oxford University Press).

Y. Lanternari, *The Religions of the Oppressed* (1963, London: Macgibbon & Kee) surveys millenarian movements throughout the world, while P. Worsley, *The Trumpet Shall Sound* (1968, 2nd ed., London: MacGibbon & Kee) and P. Lawrence, *Road Belong Cargo* (1964, Manchester: Manchester University Press) give varied explanations of the cargo cults of Melanesia.

H. A. Landsberger, *Latin American Peasant Movements* (1969, Ithaca: Cornell University Press) gives accounts of rebellions in several countries, as does R. Gott, *Guerrilla Movements in Latin America* (1970, London: Nelson). E. R. Wolf, *Peasant Wars of the Twentieth Century* (1969, New York: Harper & Row) tries specifically to show, with examples from six countries – China, Cuba, Vietnam, Algeria, Mexico, Russia – the role of various rural social categories in revolutionary activity.

Urban movements are less well documented. A number of works survey trade-union activity and useful summaries are: I. Davies, *African Trade Unions* (1966, London: Penguin Books) and R. J. Alexander, *Organised Labour in Latin America* (1965, New York: Free Press).

Too few deal with 'grass roots' unionism but a significant exception is W. H. Friedland, *Vuta Kamba: The Development of Trade Unions in Tanzania* (1969, Stanford: Hoover Institution Press). Urban violence and guerrilla movements are, for fairly obvious reasons, rarely subject to close scholarly study; but J. A. Moreno, *Barrios in Arms* (1970, Pittsburgh: Pittsburgh University Press) gives the account of fighting in Santo Domingo, capital of the Dominican republic, by a scholar-priest who set out to study urban associations but became a participant observer of guerrilla activity.

A comparative study of the role of the army is contained in: J. J. Johnson (ed.), *The Role of the Military in Underdeveloped Countries* (1962, Princeton: Princeton University Press) and M. Janowitz, *The Military in the Political Development of New Nations* (1964, Chicago: Chicago University Press). For Africa, J. M. Lee, *African Armies and Civil Order* (1969, London: Chatto & Windus) describes the development and role of the armies in the several states; R. First, *The Barrel of a Gun* (1970, London: Allen Lane The Penguin Press) is an excellent analysis of the causes and outcomes of the military coups, with special reference to Nigeria, Ghana and the Sudan. Discussions of Latin American coups abound in general works on that continent and in monographs on each country; but see, too, J. J. Johnson, *The Military and Society in Latin America* (1964, Stanford: Stanford University Press).

The very variety of revolutionary movements in recent decades has called in question the hallowed myths about the retrospective roles of urban and rural protest movements – myths which usually gave primacy to the former. Rival revolutionary political groups adhere dogmatically to the path advocated or followed by their hallowed leader – Lenin, Stalin, Mao Tse Tung or Fidel Castro. Yet the fate of

Che Guevara in Bolivia has shown how unwise it was to suppose that the methods adopted in Cuba could yield similar success elsewhere. B. Moore, *Social Origins of Dictatorship and Democracy* (1967, London: Allen Lane The Penguin Press) gives a historical dimension to the problem. In L. Huberman and P. M. Sweezy (eds.), *Regis Debray and the Latin American Revolution* (1968, New York: Monthly Review Press), a number of writers criticize the adequacy of Debray's thesis of revolution. Lastly, R. Miliband and J. Saville (eds.), *The Socialist Register 1970* (1970, London: The Merlin Press) contains an article by V. G. Kiernan 'The Peasant Revolution' which raises general issues while Basil Davidson and Eric Hobsbawm comment with African and Latin American viewpoints respectively.

Index

Abidjan, capital of Ivory Coast, 51

Accra, capital of Ghana, 51, 52; university of, 132

Achebe, Chinua (Nigeria), 129

achievement orientation, 37, 41, 70, 72

Adi-Dravidians (outcastes), in Tanjore village, 30, 31

Agbaja, Ibo village group, 27–9

age groups, in tribal societies, 35

agriculture, 46–8, 59; in Colombia, 179; in Cuba, 192; plantation, 47, 50; subsistence, 24

Ahmedabad, India, rioting in, 11

aid, from richer to poorer countries, 50, 60, 70, 197, 199

Akintola, Chief S. L. (Nigeria), 175

alienation, as characteristic of western society, 153

Aluko, Timothy (Nigeria), 129

Andhra, India: castes in, 118; Communists in, 95, 96, 157

Ankole, 45

Antioquia, province of Colombia, 71

aristocracy: in Latin America, 44, 58, 164; in peasant societies, 25, 54

armies, 55–6, 167–9, 181; coups carried out by, 56,

165–6, 169–72; mutinies in, 171

army officers: divisions between, 171; social class origins of, 167–8

Arusha Declaration, Tanzania, 196, 197, 198

Ashanti, 52

Awolowo, Chief (Nigeria), 174, 175, 176

Balewa, Sir Abubakar Tafawa (Nigeria), 175

banks: in India, 160; in Peru, 186

Bantu states, 45

Baroda University, social class origins of students at, 109

Batista, Fulgencio (Cuba), 188, 189, 190

behaviour patterns, 63; of higher castes, adopted, 117; of migrants to towns, 118; and proclaimed values, 67; and technology, 69

Belaunde, Terry (Peru), 183, 185, 186

Biafra, attempted secession of, 176–7

birth control, 59

birth-rate, and educational standard, 59

blacksmith, in Wangala, 82

Bogota, capital of Colombia: mob violence in, 180, 182; social class origins of students at University of, 140